Wicca For Beginners

Your Practical Handbook of The Wiccan Path

Discover the Secrets of Wiccan Magick and Spells and How to craft Your Book of Shadows

By Arin Corvinus

Wicca For Beginners
Your Practical Handbook of The Wiccan Path:
Discover the Secrets of Wiccan Magick and Spells
and How to craft Your Book of Shadows

Table Of Contents:

Introduction

Giving thanks to the Trees of Life lets you understand your Magick on this Earth.

Giving thanks to the roaring river and the frothy sea is what binds you to your purpose and your intentions as a person of light.

Giving thanks to the Moon and Sun and for the light they each bring is what shows you the way on your journey to enlightenment and inner peace.

Giving thanks to the abundance above and below, within and without, is what makes us all really see and know why we are here and how we are all one.

I have traveled far to discover the secrets of the craft and the essence of what it means to ask for what you want from the universe. I have celebrated many different cultural versions of witchcraft and was brought up in a family of Pagans and witches. I have learned the secrets of the Earth and Cosmos from the time I could crawl.

As I have grown in my beliefs and my power, I have learned so many valuable rituals, tools, recipes and spells that have helped me to become one with my true nature and the nature of all things alive in this universe. It is a wonderful gift to give to yourself. And as I am writing these words I feel so blessed to be sharing my knowledge of the craft with you.

Magick is for anyone who is willing to ask the bigger questions and receive honest answers. It will not suffer fools and it will always show you the correct path for YOU. Magick is a creative practice and belongs to all individuals and groups who are willing to sacrifice what they think they know in order to explore the deeper mysteries inherent in all nature.

Welcome to my guide for you, *Wicca for Beginners: Your Practical Handbook of The Wiccan Path*. In it, you will find everything you must learn to truly walk the Wiccan path and learn from your inner Magick. The tools in this book are outlined to give you the background as well as the foreground for how you can begin to work with the Magick of nature, the power of your own intuition and your psychic connection to the divine.

All of us are equipped to learn these mysteries. I have organized my own knowledge and several decades of experience into an easy to use guide to give you the foundation of Magick you need to get you started. There are so many different styles and practices of the Wiccan path and the craft. And I encourage you to choose your own Magick as you blossom into your power. This book will lovingly promote all of the possible ways you can practice and why a solitary or eclectic path can be the best choice for the creative Wiccan.

I have journeyed far to learn the benefits of both the solitary and the coven worship and will offer you the choice to decide for yourself which feels like the best path for you. This book will be a guide for those who are leaning toward a solitary practice and are looking for the steps to get started.

You will learn the history of the craft, deities of the Moon and Sun, rituals and preparations, the Wheel of the Year, the Wiccan Rede, Rule of Three, and so much more. By the time you have finished reading this guide, you will be practicing and performing your very own spells and rituals, living by the work of your craft, and manifesting all of your dreams into reality.

You will learn the steps to creating your own Book of Shadows and protecting your knowledge as you go along your path. There will be plenty of other exciting information to get you on the right track with exploring your personal Magick and as you go through this book, take time to savor the moments of teaching yourself the Wiccan way of performing the sacred and ancient art of Witchcraft.

Join me on this journey of discovery and enlightenment. All you need to bring is your curiosity and your own beautiful world of inner Magick to the table.

Enjoy the ride! So mote it be!

Chapter 1:
The World Of Paganism, Witchcraft, And Wicca

The Story Of Wiccan Origins

The real story of Wicca is not as glamorous as one might think. However, it is certainly worth hearing about the history and the knowledge of how easily a new form of worship can be formed and become one of the most popular Pagan paths you can walk today.

There is not a precise number of practicing Wiccans by consensus, but an average idea of what that number could look like is somewhere in the millions. And the numbers are growing as more and more people are able to get simple access to the Wiccan, Pagan or Shamanism Lore through the Internet.

Although they are greatly similar, they also bear certain differences and it might help you to better understand the structure of Wicca and how it came to be born in the first half of the 20th Century.

Paganism

Paganism is a somewhat broad term that can be an umbrella for a lot of practices and religions dating back to the earliest times of "witchcraft" and spirituality that was not recognized by a church organization. Paganism is the pre-Christian belief system that was largely abolished by the Christian faith, despite being the backbone of many Christian holidays and religious celebrations.

The early Pagans were open to the Magickal practice of worshipping both the divine masculine and the divine feminine and their relationship in nature. Current Pagan beliefs are a collection of wisdom from many different avenues of worship that are outside of the common religious or spiritual practices that revolve around Christ and his disciples.

The story of the Pagan religions crosses a lot of cultures and time periods and cannot be pinpointed to one specific location or era in our evolution, but was of large of influence in the development of Eastern and Western Europe around the fall of the Roman Empire and even earlier than that. Often you will find that Pagan religious holidays, feasts, and other rituals and rites tend to revolve around seasonal activities and times of the year as well as around multiple gods and goddesses, not just one central godhead figure.

Paganism can be called polytheistic or pantheistic and is usually not monotheistic. Monotheism is the worship of only one god or goddess, while polytheism allows for the presence of many divine beings and spiritual energies. Pantheism is more aligned with those who do not necessarily want to give any of the divine worship in their practice a specific name or deity to identify. But it will rather have openness towards the great spirit or divine source and sees them as the energetic presence of life force energy in all things, material and ethereal.

Fortunately, you don't really have to pick and choose with Paganism because it is such a broadly open world of spirituality that you are able to explore the possibilities. Much of what is known about the different Pagan practices and rituals from around the world is that they all somehow involve the world of nature and were directly aligned with some kind of spiritual force or deity of choice in order to invoke certain outcomes.

Paganism, like Witchcraft and Wicca, was and is, a way to manifest intentions and to present divine purpose to the great unknown. Looking at Neo-Paganism, you will still find many of the original ideas and concepts brought together from many places and cultures to give a well-rounded concept to broad terminology. It is simply divine worship that takes place in the right moments with the right intentions.

Witchcraft

Witchcraft, or simply the craft, is not to be confused with anything Satanic. Unfortunately, the practice of witchcraft is what caused a lot of unnecessary deaths, mostly that of women, in a period of Puritanism and reformation by the Catholic Church and other Christian groups.

A significant number of the women (and very few men) who were burned for these "crimes" were healers, midwives, and local wise women who were using their knowledge of herbs and their connection with nature and common sense to help and heal others.

The definition of witchcraft simply means that you are manifesting your Magickal purposes through your ability to work with certain tools, such as herbs, stones, candles, and other elementals, in order to transform the energy you are working with into what you want. In our modern times, many people refer to this as the Law of Attraction, popularized by a New York Times Bestseller called, *The Secret.*

I am certain that many of the men and women reading that book when it was released weren't thinking in their heads, "Oh yeah, this sounds just like witchcraft!" In fact, one of the main realities of practicing witchcraft is that you use your own inner power along with your chosen set of tools to manifest what you are looking for in your life through the Law of Attraction.

The fun part of witchcraft is the casting of spells and performing rituals, and there is always so much more to it than that. Our stereotype as a culture or society of what a witch looks like is an old woman with a big, hooked nose covered in warts, riding her broom around a cauldron. It was the common idea of witches even though a majority of the women burned at the stake were between the ages of 12 and 30 years of age.

A cauldron is a common tool for casting spells and practicing witchcraft but it was also really just a cooking pot that most families owned. Everyone had a cauldron and it was the witch who made it famous for what she could do within it or how she was able to make her own Magick using a common pot.

Witchcraft really is like brewing a soup in a big pot, metaphorically speaking. You use a set of ingredients and a recipe on the right night of the year under a certain moon and you find yourself glowing with the light of your Magickal elixir, concocted to revitalize you in the chilly winter months.

Another example would be the empowering of the self and the realization of certain things from within you that you seek to draw out. Witchcraft is a very personal experience and it has been for everyone since it naturally began. We are naturally drawn to doing these types of things in order to connect with our own inner nature and power and so witchcraft is a source of knowing your own divinity and power.

The value of witchcraft is that it has always given a person or a group the opportunity to communicate with the self and the source of creation. The practice itself- the rituals, spells, and incantations- is what we do to pick up the telephone and talk to the universe about what we want to conjure or manifest. It isn't always just for the self, either. Many of those who practice witchcraft are working hard to heal the wounds of Mother Earth by asking for deeper peace and harmony amongst cultures and groups. Others are working to help the environment by showing up for it in a way that works with the craft.

Witchcraft is a dynamic practice that is available to anyone. It is a creative and artistic process that allows you to build upon the energy of your life, or transform it into something else. The history behind it is long, likely longer than historians and archaeologists are even able to document or prove.

As witchcraft has evolved, it has also remained the same. It is a simple effort and has never really been an exact science because it has never needed to be. It is versatile and Universal and treats us all well if we treat it well in return. Some Shamans have been referred to as "witch doctors" implying that they use witchcraft to connect to the Magick of healing others. Like Paganism and Witchcraft, Shamanism has its own background and identity and plays a very similar part.

Shamanism

Shamanism does not belong to a specific culture. It hasn't been around with us for as long as the Pagan religions, according to some sources, however, it is certainly as old, or even older, according to others. It is almost impossible to determine the origins of

Shamanism. The common misconception that it comes only from Native American tribes has led many people to consider it from that perspective, when in fact there is South and Central American Shamanism as well as Celtic and Siberian Shamanism.

Shamanism is a practice that stems from a desire to walk the path of healer and Medicine Man or Woman. It is often seen in families or tribes as a practical gift that is either passed down from parent to child, or you are chosen and trained with an already experienced Shaman. Some people have this innately within them and even if you are not a part of a culture or group that has a Shaman, you may be led down the path of becoming one anyway because of your hidden gifts to work with this kind of energy.

Shamanism is a personal quest for spiritual knowledge in order to help the self and to help other people. Shamanic culture and practice is one that will use the spirituality of the environment and its creatures, landscapes, and peoples in order to affect change. Shamans have a very close connection to the spirit world and are a lot better able to communicate with the divine than many other people are. It is a challenging role to be in a direct link to the nature of spirit and so it is a harder path to walk.

As I have learned from my own Shamanic path, I would suggest that if you are looking to work in the world of Spirit, make sure you are prepared for the lessons that are offered. You cannot simply declare yourself Shaman; you must go through many challenging tests and periods of growth to truly know what you can say to others from the voice of Spirit.

Shamanism embraces all people and all energies and is willing to look at both the light and the dark for greater balance and integrity in asking for what you truly want from Spirit. Wicca has a little bit of all of these things involved in its origin and so as you move forward into the History of Wicca, understand how these three realms of Magick play a part.

History Of Wicca

Wicca is not an old religion by compared to many of the other topics we have already covered. It was originally brought to the surface as a way to allow for modern Witchcraft to have its Renaissance and was done so around the time of the 1940s and 50s.

One man has been credited as the "Father" of Wicca, but it wouldn't be fair to only credit him. There were certainly other people involved in this craft that are responsible for the formation and organization of this practice.

Gerald Gardner, the Father of Wicca, was a British civil servant who had long been curious about archeology and folklore as well as Spiritualism and Occult matters. When he was inducted into the New Forest coven at the end of the 1930s he was greatly influenced by the practice of Witchcraft and other Pagan rituals and rites. Eventually, he broke off to form his own coven, Bricket Wood and was there able to formalize his perspective on "Witch-cult" practices.

There were certainly others that aided in the formation of what we now know as Wicca, but even then, no one really called it that. The word 'wica' was used as a term to describe the members of the craft, being the Old-English/Anglo-Saxon word for wise people and sorcerers. It wasn't until the Bricket Wood coven spread their knowledge and ideas to Australia and North America that it adopted the name.

The tools of Wicca were brought together from Pagan ritual, occult practices like those written about by Aleister Crowley, and even some Freemasonry ideas and rituals. A major component was the worship of nature and the God and Goddess. According to the philosophy of Wicca, the

God and Goddess are totally equal and live in celebration of that balance, part of what Wicca worships during the Wheel of the Year. This idea was virtually unheard of in the patriarchal society and world religions of that time and even of the present.

Wicca celebrates the Pagan ways, the elements of Witchcraft, the aspects and pathways of Shamanism, and various other occult spirituality. It was born out of the principles and beliefs that we are all Magickal and that our fortune lies in embracing the divinity of nature through our connection to the God and Goddess.

Of course, Gardnerian Wicca was only the beginning and it has since evolved into many other possible paths. There are no real rules, just ethics and guidelines to help you practice with a good heart, mind, and spirit. Wicca establishes many benefits to the individual as well as to the group and the next section will explain that in greater detail.

Benefits Of Practicing Wicca

Wicca wasn't necessarily invented in order to benefit the individual in the ways that I am about to talk about. The purpose of it was to practice witchcraft and celebrate the God and the Goddess and to involve all the rhythms and cycles of nature into the worship of daily life. Many of the benefits I will tell you about are only some of the ways that we as a modern culture have learned to look out our personal health from the perspective of mind, body, and spirit.

The wholeness we are all seeking is easily achieved through the practice of Wicca because of how it works with you and your energy as you manifest your dreams and desires. When I was younger going through my own exploration of how I wanted to work with Magick, I was certainly not very good at caring for myself like I am now. It is a part of our journey to discover the way we take care of ourselves as we leave the nests of our parents and fly free on our own.

I did have a profound relationship with a master teacher at that time and learned a lot more working with Wicca than I did with any other Magickal practice. I had to live a life in which I cared for myself well in order to practice Magick well and the results were wonderful and deeply transformative. In this book, I have attempted to illustrate the main benefits of practicing Wicca to better live your life and understand your purpose in the grand scheme of all things.

- **Spiritual Health**

  Spirituality is one of the main causes for most people to engage with a practice like Wicca. A lot of people are trying to get away from organized religions that will ask them to sacrifice who they are as an individual to better fit in with the "group mentality". So many Pagans and witches I know have lived a life of spiritual discord because they felt untrue to themselves in these types of religious settings.

Wicca is a balance between the self and the divine and empowers the individual to embrace their unique qualities as well as to embrace their essential participation in the evolution of all things in nature. The greatest benefit I have found through the worship of Wiccan beliefs and practices is the spiritual closeness with nature and her rhythms that keep me in my healthiest state of mind with the life I choose to lead.

The answers to your questions about your spirituality are a part of the seeking you will do when you engage with a path of Magick. There are no doctrines or harsh rules that force you to believe only one thing. It is a much more dynamic and open-minded form of spirituality that can allow you to be equally open-minded to all other parts of the universe at once.

- **Self-Care**

Self-Care may not sound like a magical benefit of Wicca, but as it happens it is one of the most important parts of understanding the laws of nature and of the self. Wicca supports a life of balance and harmony and will always ask you to take stock of where you are with your own energy and purpose in your life.

It is not something you are required to do to practice Wicca, however, it certainly does make a huge difference when you realize that so much of the Magick you perform will help you improve your personal well-being, both within and without. Self-Care means a lot of different things to a lot of different people. In Wicca, it simply means that you are creating a healthy balance on all levels of self.

Wicca asks you to be present with your energy in a way that you may have never been before and so it offers a great transformation to develop new ways of caring for yourself then you have felt before. It is best to perform all your spells and rituals with grounded and balanced energy so that you are not negatively impacting your Magick practices with negative thoughts and low vibrations. Self-Care takes you toward your highest self and that is what Wicca is all about.

- **Creativity**

Wicca is a creative practice. Sure, you can look at someone else's Grimoire or Book of Shadows and copy their spells, but you can also just intuitively create your own from the energy of your life and yourself. If you are in a coven you will work with a group to create Magick, which is an incredibly powerful experience. Collaboration with other witches feels even more powerful and you can really feel the energy you are creating together as you manifest.

It is also wonderful for self-expression, whether you are in a coven, or solitary. The practice of Wicca allows for a lot of room to get creative and be artistic in the way that you create your altar or build your book of Shadows. You are the one with the authority to perform your rituals and spells in a way that feels best for you and your Magickal intentions.

The benefits of having a creative license over your craft are that you gain confidence in your knowledge, your intuition, and your personal power in a whole lot of ways. It doesn't matter what you do to make a spell work as long as you are trusting that what you are doing is the right path for your craft. The word 'craft' from witchcraft is also the word the comes from crafting something into existence. Your hobbies might include knitting, sewing, sculpting, or painting. Did you ever think about how art is itself incredibly Magickal?

The benefits of creativity are always available, whether they are for modern hobby crafts, or for the Magick you cast in your circle at your altar.

- **Meditation**

It is scientifically proven that meditation is good for everyone. It connects you to your mind, body, and spirit on all levels and helps you attain a higher state of awareness while it promotes physical health. Meditation is often linked to spirituality and its many practices and you may not think it would be involved in the Wiccan practice, but it is one of the main attributes.

In almost every spell and ritual I perform, there is a moment of meditation. I have to meditate in order to connect with my inner knowing and the divine source energy I am working with. It only takes a few moments and it brings me into deeper closeness with the energy of all things, providing me with the ultimate balance.

Meditation isn't something you have to teach yourself how to do well; it comes naturally during your craftwork and if you are simply open to being with yourself and your Magick, then you are in meditation. Overall, meditation is just a natural part of communing with your own soul as well as the soulful energy present in all things in life.

- **Kindness**

This may not seem like a likely benefit, but as you learn more about the principles of Wicca in future chapters, you will understand that the ethics of Magick ask that you are mindful of not hurting anyone. The goal of Wicca or any kind of Magick is to empower and transform and not to cause pain or harm.

There are some witches and wizards who practice darker Magick and have their own reasons for doing so, and as you study Magick it is important that you learn the difference between these balancing forces. In my practice, I always wish to exercise energy of kindness because I trust the laws of karmic retribution and that any energy you cast can return to you three-fold.

From the perspective of Wicca, it doesn't mean that you are just being kind to your fellow human. You are also asked to be kind to every rock, and pebble, every tree, and shrub, every bird and snake. We are in a mighty web of life and the circles of life, death and rebirth are always present with us. Exercising kindness is a natural law of Wicca that shows you to have presence and awareness with all things around you which leads to an even deeper kindness and respect for the self.

You will surely find even more elements of Wicca that are beneficial to you and your life. It will come with practice. And as you practice you will find that all of the Magick involved with your path will lead you to a greater feeling of wholeness with an attitude of awareness like you have never known before.

Coven, Circle, Solitary, Eclectic

Before we continue on to the next chapters about the beliefs and practices of Wicca, let's take a look at the different ways that people practice.

- **Coven**

  A Coven is a group of witches who come together to practice Magick as a group. In Wiccan practices, there are usually 13 members often including a High Priest and a High Priestess. The Coven will come together regularly for rituals and rites on Sabbats and Esbats to celebrate the Wheel of the Year. They may come together for other spells and rituals not related to the seasonal shifts and will usually operate from a shared Book of Shadows.

- **Circle**

A circle is much less formal than a Coven and will involve anywhere from three to 10 members. More than that can get too out of hand and disagreeable. There aren't usually any High Priests or Priestesses to govern the circle rituals and so it is more about coming together to celebrate similar interests in Magick. This will also often relate to celebrating the Wheel of the Year and will open up to an even larger group for bigger parties and celebrations. It is more about the social aspect of having like-minded people to enjoy Full Moon Esbats, Solstices and Equinoxes with.

- **Solitary**

A solitary practitioner of Wicca will usually follow a specific tradition or belief system but will do it on their own without the work of being involved in a coven. It is often the choice of those who are very open-minded to their own work and have more specific needs and intentions to focus on that would not be available to them as easily if they were only in a coven.

Some solitary Wiccans will be coven members and will also practice the coven beliefs on their own at home, while other solitaries will choose to invoke their preferred form of worship through their own timing and personal practice and Magickal purposes.

- **Eclectic**

  An eclectic practitioner will usually have no fixed practice or intention to only fit into one kind of belief system but will incorporate many deities, structures, symbols, and Magickal practices. It is less uniform and much more creative and open-ended. It can be a great choice for those who need to explore a lot of different aspects of Wiccan culture and witchcraft before initiating oneself into any particular order.

There isn't a right or a wrong way to choose your path and you may have to evolve with it as you grow. For many beginning witches and Wiccans, a solitary path is the best choice so that you can become more closely connected to your own Magick before you commit to a circle or a coven. I have definitely embraced all of the different forms of practices and I fully enjoyed being a solitary practitioner as my way of self-discovery in the adventure.

This book is geared toward those beginners who are working from a solitary, or eclectic path, but with an open-heartedness for anyone who is wishing to find the right coven or circle on their path.

The next chapter will begin the journey of Wicca by talking about the deities of the Moon and Sun and why the God and Goddess are such an important aspect to the worship of nature in Wicca.

Chapter 2: The Deities Of The Moon And Sun

Wicca elaborates on a Universal concept present in all cultures, religions, and artifacts: the presence of the divine feminine and the divine masculine and the eternal balance between them. Not all people would agree that there is a balance between the Mother and Father energy of our world and they wouldn't be totally wrong.

There is a great internal and external battle that is seeking the balance between the patriarchal reality we have engaged with for so many centuries and the matriarchal bounty that was present in many civilizations before the great push of masculinity took hold. There are many opinions to present on that subject, I could write an entirely separate book about it!

Within the coursework of learning traditional Wicca, it is important to open-mindedly research the quality of energy inherent in the masculine and feminine forces of nature. It isn't always just about the female or male gender; in fact, it is often more about the energy of the male and female bond that is worshipped in Wicca.

The main practices of Gardnerian Wicca and other forms of Pagan worship embrace the relationship between the Goddess energy and her Male counterpart, as they connect to each other to create life on Earth. The Wheel of the Year is the story of these divine energies as they consummate a marriage of equals to give birth to the Spring and Summer bounty that feeds us through the cold winter months.

The deities of Goddess and God are most notably represented by the Moon and the Sun in Wicca. And so all of the rituals, Sabbats, and Esbats pertain to these ideas and concepts. To help you see the rich story of elemental creation between these two, powerful and necessary forces, I will break down the concepts of the God and Goddess to show you their relevance to Wiccan ritual and belief.

The Goddess And The God

The Goddess and God have been depicted in a variety of ways in many different forms and cultural ideations. In Wicca, there is a great story of both deities that demonstrates their rhythms and cycles as they go through the cycle of life, death, and rebirth.

The Goddess is represented in three forms and will often be referred to as the Triple Goddess. She grows in her wisdom through the cycles of the year. She is first the Maiden, preparing for life in her ethereal womb, followed by the Mother, full of life and fecundity represented by the Earth's bounty, and finally the Crone, as the green things of the season's light fade and die, leaving the wise old woman to reflect on her dying light.

As the year shifts into new energy and a new beginning, so too is the Maiden reborn and released into her next cycle of life, death, and rebirth.

As with the Triple Goddess, the Male God goes on a similar journey, beginning as a youth and growing into a virile and procreative man who gives to the creation of all life on Earth with his power and life force energy. As the seasons change into decay, the Male God experiences his "Autumn years" before passing into an underworld and darkness before beginning again as the youth of New Year.

There are hundreds, and possibly thousands of different forms of Goddess and God that have been seen in a variety of beliefs and cultures. Many Celtic and Asian myths and legends have given birth to some of the more popular deities that are represented, and it will really depend on your chosen path that determines which form(s) you choose to work with and worship.

In traditional Wicca, the differences between the Goddess and God can be seen in their most profound forms. The Moon and the Sun are the ancient symbols of Paganism, Witchcraft and other Shamanistic paths that represent the female and male forms of divinity. They each have their own energy and interpretation that is a Universal truth in most cultures.

The Moon And The Sun

The Moon is the symbol of the Goddess while the sun represents the energy of the God. The two are separate but equally important to the cycles and rhythms of life. As you will read in this section there is a powerful balance that Wiccans celebrate on a daily basis, as well as during the Sabbats and Esbats of the Wheel of the Year.

The Moon is the waters of emotion, compassion, empathy, and sacred love. The Moon is also associated with intuition, psychic ability, clairvoyance, as well as nightmares, lunacy and bad dreams. Many women have been called "hysterical" in history and there was a lot of connection to the idea that women are more emotional than men, giving a closer association to the energy of the moon and the "condition of women to have menses." The Moon is not biased of course, and both men and women possess female energy and vice versa.

The Moon is the energy of the night. She is the kind offering of light in the black sky in her fullness, and the dark force of quiet contemplation when she is completely shadowed and "New". The Moon has often been associated with feminine energy because of the connection to the cycles of womanhood, especially menstruation.

Many women today still use the moon as their number one source of connection to the divine during their "periods" and cycles of internal life, death, and rebirth. The Moon pulls the tides of the oceans and has a major impact on all life on Earth. The magnetism of this celestial orb is powerful and brilliant and comes to us through a 28-day cycle every month of the calendar year.

The Moon is the Triple Goddess and when you consider the phases of the Moon, you will understand what I mean. Beginning with a New Moon, you have the energy of the Maiden. She is waxing and full of potential as she grows her passions, desires, and intentions to come to fullness. The Full Moon is the Mother energy of the Triple Goddess form. As she enters her fullness, you can feel the powerful energy of her persuasion to give birth to all that has been gestating from the time of the Maiden Moon.

After the Full Moon, we enter the waning period, the Winter years of the Mother as she becomes a Crone woman and goes within to reflect on her time of fullness and birth, before being reborn again on the coming New Moon. This cycle is a part of the energy of the Goddess and can be celebrated in the monthly cycles of womanhood, as well as throughout the course of the year with the nature of the Sun God.

The Sun is the powerful, bright light of day that shines white and hot in the height of Summer. It can burn and scorch and it can also bring life and abundance. The Sun, like the Moon, goes through a yearly course of waxing and waning. The Moon repeats this cycle monthly while the distant Sun is fixed and as we travel around it and rotate on our axis, we engage with the seasons of change inherent in the cycle of our journey around the Sun.

The Sun is at its weakest leading up to the Winter Solstice before the great shift happens and the days start to increase in length. The increasing length of the day means that the Sun God is staying longer in the sky and growing into his strength. He transforms into his most powerful form of "manhood" at the height of Summer when the Sun is highest in the sky and the days are the longest.

The Sun is born as a boy on Yule which is the celebration that marks the longest night of the year. As the year ends and turns into a new calendar year, the boy of the last days of Winter grows into the young man of Spring, the Green Man, who prepares to unite with the Maiden Goddess energy. By May, the Sun God and the Goddess "consummate" their marriage and begin to sow the seeds of Earth's abundance.

The Oak King of Summer is one with the Mother energy, before they both begin to shift. After the Summer Solstice, the Sun will start his waning journey into the Autumn years of his life and will release himself to the age of the "dying man" becoming the spiritual wise one, often called the Holly King. Like the Crone Goddess the time of the lowest light in the Autumn, before winter shifts the light, is when the God succumbs to darkness and death before his rebirth at Yule once more.

As you can see, the Sun and Moon both represent the energy of the Goddess and God. And although the Triple Goddess is always present in the yearly cycle beside the Sun, she is also constantly going through her own unique cycle every month. They are both the cause of why we continue to exist in this great cycle of life, death, and rebirth. But they are more than just the cycles of the Sun and Moon.

The Goddess and the God represent an even deeper life force as depicted by the divine feminine and the divine masculine in all people. It is the great balance of the two that we are all seeking as individuals.

Divine Feminine And Divine Masculine

The feminine and masculine are not about gender. You can easily divide things into a gender difference, but in Wicca, we are always looking for equality between opposing forces and the balance of those forces within the self.

The divine masculine and the divine feminine do not speak of the gender of male and female forms but rather the energy of each in their most symbolic forms. Some women are more masculine, and some men are more feminine by nature. It is this natural form that causes us to choose not to box in or pigeon-hold the ideas of masculinity and femininity when dealing with Wiccan Magick.

The divine masculine is the collective unconscious energy of the male, or masculine life force energy present in all things, while the divine feminine is the collective unconscious female life force energy present in all things. To suggest that this is only male or female as gender is too confining to the world of Magick.

So what does that even mean? The male life force energy is white light, ambitious, forceful, logical, positive, powerful, direct, fast, hot, dry, hard, and aggressive energy. The female life force energy is dark, gentle, negative, emotive, connective, intuitive, reaction, contemplation, rebirth, openness, slow, wet, yielding, and passive energy. As you can see, they are essentially opposing forces and that is part of what Wicca is celebrating in the course of a year, or even in the course of a ritual or spell.

Some Magick needs more divine masculine energy, while other Magick needs the forces of the feminine divine. Again this doesn't mean gendered energy. It is representative of the symbolic energy of each force. Think of the Chinese Yin-Yang symbols which show the sacred balance of these elemental forces. It opens you to understanding that within each of us there is a sacred balance of both.

As a woman I'm considered or judged because of my gender. But as I see it, I may be represented in the physical form by my feminine body, but I am always looking for an internal energetic balance with my male animus as well as my female animus. The animus is the sacred energy of my spirit that has to seek complete balance to create wholeness from within. This is the act I perform in my Magick and keeps me equivalent with both the Goddess and the God, the Moon and the Sun, the divine feminine and the divine masculine.

As you look for your own internal balance through the concepts of the deities of the Moon and Sun, explore how you are both in your own world. Are you ambitious and direct, logical and fast in some parts of your world, while you are soft and gentle, intuitive and yielding in others? Or are you strictly one or the other? Bring it into focus as you pursue your path and consider what ways you will enjoy bringing balance to your own sacred energy through the worship of the Goddess and the God in Wicca.

The next chapter will help you decide your path, if you haven't already, by expanding upon the different forms of Wicca as it has evolved with our different cultural explorations. There will be plenty

of ways to choose your path and this next chapter
will help you feel better informed about which path
you may want to travel.

Chapter 3: Choose Your Wiccan Path

Wicca allows you to explore your path in a lot of different ways. Not all Wiccans choose a specific path (Eclectic) and prefer to incorporate a variety of these following concepts and ideas into their unique practices. For any solitary Wiccan, you can determine what style of Wicca resonates the most with you and find out where you want to explore and practice.

Many of the Wiccans that I know and have met over the years have also started with one path and gone to another after years of exploring one version of it. The key thing to remember is that Wicca is a creative reality and that all of us have the right at any time to explore other opportunities and options.

As you begin to take this adventure, you may want a good place to begin and the following styles of Wicca may help you decide the best place for you to start your practice. I myself have created my own rituals and coven practices that are specific to my unique journey with a variety of these methods, which would classify me as Eclectic. But I am also accepting of not being classified in any form of worship and prefer only to be called Wiccan.

The beautiful thing is that you can choose your direction and your journey as you get closer to your intuition. The ones that resonate the most with you are calling out to you for a reason, so just go with it and honor your truth! If you decide that none of these paths feels just right for you, then you might want to explore the path of the Solitary Eclectic.

Gardnerian Wicca

You have already learned the very brief history of Wicca and its origins with a man by the name of Gerald Garner. He is considered the "Father" or

"Grandfather" of all Wicca, however, there are many others that claim another origin citing that the umbrella word for Wicca described a wide variety of practices that were forming all at once.

His original path with Witchcraft began in the New Forest Coven where he learned many of his skills from the High Priestess 'Old Dorothy' Clutterbuck. After his own coven, Bricket Wood formed, he began to publish several books, including novels, about the form of spirituality he was practicing. According to some sources, it wasn't until 1951 that the last laws against practicing Witchcraft were finally repealed in England which then saw the rise of this particular 'religion'; especially the then-popular form of Witchcraft being promoted by Gardner and his coven members.

It has been described as being very traditional and stemming from a long lineage of initiation and inheriting the secrets of the coven in practice. Usually, a High Priestess is always in charge, and a

High Priest will also sometimes be present or involved in much of the ceremonial rituals and castings. There is a shared Book of Shadows that is used by the coven members who when initiated will usually have to make their own copy by hand, word for word. Additions and improvisations are accepted, as long as the original Book is preserved in its fullness. It is considered to be very secretive and hierarchal, revealing very little about what goes on behind closed doors.

Most Gardnerian covens will be autonomous and led by the High Priestess/High Priest (HPS/HP) and they will also receive guidance from the HPS/HP who trained them and are usually operating in another coven. Covens branch off and create a coven-hive that are part of a great family tree and lineage of Wiccans.

Some basic beliefs include the Wiccan Rede (Harm None) as well as reincarnation. Covens tend to be arranged in couples of male/female. This way there are even numbers of each in order to increase and accomplish the interaction of the balance of male and female energy (Sun and Moon deities). This is also referred to as the Lord and Lady in Gardnerian Wicca. Ceremonies of male/female balance will often include chanting, dancing, singing, mandatory nudity, and so forth.

A majority of Gardnerian traditions will have three degrees in a coven, moving from initiate all the way up to HPS/HP. The HPS/HP is responsible for organizing the coven gatherings as well as training their inductees and coven members. The main role is to conduct the rituals and circles and preserve the Book of Shadows to carry on to the next HPS/HP.

Essentially, if you want to walk the path of Gardnerian Wicca, you will need to find a coven that is already practicing and looking for initiates in order to learn the deeper secrets, rites, and rituals. Some of what is known about this style of Wicca was published by Gardner in his many publications, much of which was thought to have come from the first coven he was involved with. He is said to have added a lot more to those practices and Doreen Valiente is credited for authoring much of the popular Book of Shadows that was published under this form of Wiccan practice.

The secrets of Gardnerian Wicca are kept by the coven. To explore it further, you may want to dig more deeply into that journey with a coven in your community. This way you can learn that path from the High Priestess/High Priest.

Alexandrian Wicca

The Alexandrian path is considered to be very similar to the Gardnerian path with just a few things that separate them from each other. According to my own research and experiences, the Alexandrian Wiccans use the athame as a tool to represent the element of fire and the wand to represent the element of air, while Gardnerian Wiccans will use them oppositely.

It was originally created by a man named Alex Sanders who claimed to have been an initiate of Witchcraft by his Grandmother in the 1930s. The name for this practice does not, in fact, come from his name of Alex, but from Ancient Alexandria. The rituals are formal and traditional with a heavy emphasis on the dramas played out within the Wheel of the Year between the male and female deities and their polarization. Similar in its practices to Gardnerian Wicca, Alexandrian Wicca will usually fall into a more eclectic category and does not require mandatory nudity during some ceremonies and rituals.

Dianic Wicca

There are said to be two distinct branches of Dianic Wicca and so I will refer to them separately as Branch One and Branch Two.

Branch One was originally founded in Texas by two people named Morgan McFarland and Mark Roberts. This form of Wicca will give precedence and primary authority to the Goddess and will honor the Horned God (Male God) as a consort, but not necessarily as her counterpart in balance. Covens of Branch One are a mix of men and women and tend to fully embrace the practice of honoring the divine feminine overall. But they will also honor the male aspect as part of her sacred engagement in the Wheel of life.

Branch Two is often referred to as "Feminist Dianic Wicca or Witchcraft" and is exclusive to worshipping the Goddess and the divine feminine. This branch of Dianic Wicca is comprised of women-only covens and circles (or solitaries). They have a less hierarchical structure compared to the Gardnerian and Alexandrian Wicca paths and are based in community decision making rather than High Priestess authority. This branch focuses on communication, feminism, emotional support, and so forth. There is said to be a strong lesbian presence in this branch of Wicca but is of course not exclusive in this way. It is only exclusive to women.

The Church Of Wicca

The Church of Wicca and was formed by Gavin and Yvonne Frost. It is the most patriarchal of the Wiccan practices and has only recently begun to involve the Goddess in their traditional deity structure. This style of Wicca actually refers to itself as "Baptist Wicca". It has sometimes been referred to as "Celtic Wicca" but there are other practices of Wicca that are more aligned with Celtic deities. Especially the Celtic Goddesses are more aligned with a Celtic belief system and path.

It may have a touch of Celtic symbolism and structure involved in it, but is more of a "high magic" traditional practice that leans eclectic. They will usually use three circles for casting instead of one, common to other Wiccan practices. The circles are built with sulfur, herbs, and salt, with runes and symbols cast between them. There is a choice of using only a white-handled athame, while most other traditions call for a black-handled athame.

Georgian Wicca

Georgian Wicca is best described as being an eclectic practice and was founded by a man named George Patterson whose main source of empowering his circles of magic was the phrase, "If it works, use it. If it doesn't, don't"; meaning that rather than have a set code for only one form of practice or tradition, he believed in exploring the possibilities.

Much of the material offered to students of Georgian Wicca appeared to be largely Alexandrian, apart from this eclectic mindset and belief held by Patterson. The tradition of Georgian Wicca seemed to have a variety of followers and the founder himself had a lot of contributions to make to the Wiccan news of the day. Typically, you could just call Georgian Wicca and eclectic treatment of Gardnerian and Alexandrian paths with a dash of something extra from George: use the Magick if it works, and don't if it doesn't.

Discordianism

Discordianism is basically an agreement with Magick that there are definitely powerful forces out there that must create chaos in order for a balance to exist in nature. Think of the joker or jester, always working to make a joke out of the misery and sorrow of life.

According to Discordianism, the absurd is as valuable and necessary as the mundane and therefore there must be humor and there must be chaos to balance order. It can be a liberating journey for anyone who has always walked a path of order. Even for those who are dabbling in working with all of the other paths, it is important to remember the balance created by a path like Discordianism which embraces the opposing forces of all things in nature, choosing the side of the joker, jester or chaos maker.

These somewhat similar and also distinctly different forms of Wicca are worth looking into more deeply. Some of them require a coven, while you can also take the concepts and apply them to your own eclectic practice. For the solitary practitioner, any of these models of Wicca can be embraced and you can also choose none of them and create your own version of it to work with.

It helps to have an idea of what they are all promoting to decide where you might lean if you were in a group or a circle, or even on your own at home in front of your personal altar. You certainly don't have to choose your path today. And you may need to spend some time getting better acquainted with the practice of witchcraft, casting Magick and performing rituals before you decide what to fully embrace on your journey.

The next chapter will give you more information about the rituals performed and what they actually look like, step-by-step. I will be using a fairly traditional explanation but keeping it a general process so that it can be viewed from any kind of Wiccan approach.

Chapter 4:
Rituals And Their Preparation

Wiccan rituals and rites are the reason for a coven or a witch to come to a place of gathering power and celebrate something important. Even if that importance is just the mystery of life, the God and Goddess, and the self. The rituals and rites of many Wiccan practices are not easy to replicate. A majority of covens are secretive about their practices and very few of them will perform them in a public setting to be viewed.

Rituals will differ greatly among different covers depending on the coven's practice and Book of Shadows. For a solitary practitioner, rituals and rites can be very personal and creative and will provide them with a lot of connection to their personal power and Magick. All rituals and rites will usually follow some specific steps in order to embrace the ritual aspect of connecting to the divine and creating the proper ceremony around the intended purpose for celebration.

Taking what you already know about Wicca and its various paths, you can look at this chapter on ritual preparations and get an idea from the different styles of practice how each one might hold a ceremony a little differently. For example, the second Branch of Dianic Wicca will have a representation of the Goddess only in their rituals and rites. While Gardnerian Wiccans may dance around a fire in the nude to celebrate consummation between the God and Goddess for theirs.

Giving up the secrets of rituals is not something a true witch would usually do, and no two rites are performed the same way from coven to coven, and solitary to solitary. Remember that Wicca is creative and so are the ceremonies that revolve around your practice.

Wiccan Rituals And Rites

One of the major ways that Wiccans will celebrate through rituals is on the Sabbats and Esbats during the Wheel of the Year. These special and specific holidays mark important moments in the cycles of our own journeys as well as the relationship between the Goddess and the God through the Seasons. The Esbats are rituals to honor phases of the Moon and are most frequently observed on Full Moons and Dark Moons.

Not all rituals have to pertain to the Wheel of the Year and the calendar of Lunar phases and the cycle of the Triple Goddess. Other rituals can be about honoring other deities or specific moments in life that are more personal and will bring more abundance and prosperity to the coven or solitary. Some rituals are more like spells and crafting them is just as important a ritual as invoking the God and the Goddess on Ostara or Beltane.

Many of the rituals that a Wiccan will perform will relate to nature, elemental Magick, and the energy of various spells and manifestations. The point of the ritual is that you create a sacred space to conjure Magick or call upon the Goddess and God to witness your powers so that you can be a part of the great circle of life. Rituals are essentially an act of communication with the Great Divine with the use of specific tools and a variation of certain steps that keep you aligned with your Magickal purposes.

Other Wiccan ceremonies, also known as 'rites', are what we might collectively refer to as 'rites of passage' that are significant or important moments in a person's, family's or coven's life. Some rites of passage include the following:

- Wiccaning- when a baby is born to a member of the craft, this ceremony welcomes them but does not obligate them to choose this path until they are ready to decide for themselves.

- Dedication- a ceremony or rite for someone who is confirming their personal interest in the craft they are choosing to practice.

- Initiation- this is usually a powerful moment for a person to become reborn into Wicca. It is a symbolic death of the "old self", to embrace the "new self" as Wiccan. Many will adopt a new name for their initiation.

- Hand-Fasting- this rite of passage marks the marriage of two people through a Wiccan union ceremony. Originally it was said to only last for one year, but today it is considered to be a permanent and legal bond or marriage to a partner.

- Parting of the Ways- this rite will recognize the end of a marriage and allow for a symbolic and literal parting and end of matrimony. It is usually a relaxed and easy-going celebration which is not as common as the more common system of divorce in our culture. This rite allows for a blessing of both souls to go on in love and happiness.

- Funeral Rite- the end of the life of a Wiccan who is celebrated the Wiccan way at the end of their physical life. Wiccan believe in reincarnation and so there is a lot of preparation for their soul to return to a new life when the time is right.

These rites of passage are a part of the rituals of Wicca and are often created to be unique to the individuals who are being celebrated as well as through the unique quality of the coven or practice. The tools and ingredients used will vary widely and could pertain to what point in the Wheel of the Year you are in when any of these rites would be performed.

Another notable rite that is a powerful and potent journey is called "The Great Rite" which celebrates the sexual union between the God and the Goddess, which begins in Spring around the time of Beltane. It celebrates what life comes forward from the Earth to be harvested in the future days.

Wiccans are notoriously sex-positive and although some covens will actually perform sex rites within their rituals, most will only symbolically recreate the element of sexual union between the Goddess and God as they consummate their sacred marriage to bring more life to the Earth.

Usually, the Great Rite will begin with a sharing of food and drink, followed by a ceremony in which a male coven member will hold the athame while a female coven member will hold and display the chalice. These are the sacred symbols of male and female energy. The chalice is usually filled with water or wine, or another concoction or brew. The male will hold the athame above the chalice with the blade pointed downward, preparing to enter it.

An incantation and invocation are usually spoken to bring the power of the Goddess and the God into the presence of the ritual and to help them join together in their sacred union through the symbolic gesture of lowering the athame into the chalice and wetting the blade with the sacred waters of the feminine cup.

As long as there are people practicing Wicca and Witchcraft, there will be rites and rituals performed. It is what we do! And it always a good feeling to be supported by the Magick of these practices. Some circles will recreate epic drums between God and Goddess, like a play in a theater, while others will simply perform certain symbolic gestures with their sacred tools and words of invocation. It really is a matter of your own personal choices with your solitary craft, or what your coven is performing regularly as a group. The standard steps to a majority of Wiccan rituals can be seen in the next section.

The Steps Of Wiccan Ritual

There are 8 steps to a Wiccan ritual. Bear in mind that depending on your coven, or your own solitary practice, these steps might alter or change and that's okay. It is a general guideline to help you see an overview of the steps involved in the Wiccan rituals and rites of passage. In Chapter 7, I will go into further detail about how to cast your own circle of Magick and set up your altar. But for now, these simple steps are a good rule of thumb for any Magick ritual you are going to perform.

Purification Of The Self

Purification of the self is the first big step to any ritual. If you think about it, all day long you are probably doing normal, everyday tasks and chores, interacting with the world and lots of people, or dealing with things far less Magickal. You can absorb and collect a lot of unwanted energies that you definitely don't want to carry into your Magick spells and rituals.

Purification of your energy and your body is a way to prepare yourself for what is in store. It can be a powerful grounding technique to help you relax and let go of some of the mundane issues of life before you step into your circle of Magick.

The most popular methods for purifying the self are purification baths and smudging. Purification baths don't have to be a fully elaborate ritual and can be as simple as lighting some spell candles and adding some salt to your water before you step into the tub and relax. You don't have to be in the bath for very long either. 5-10 minutes in warm-hot saltwater with candles is plenty of time for purification. After your bath, you would need to dress in your ritual clothing and immediately begin your next steps to the ritual.

Smudging is also an effective way to purify your body and can be done in the space you are planning to work. It is an easy way to release any unwanted energies from your being so that you are a pure channel for Magick to occur. The most common type of smudging herb is white sage. It has been used by many different cultures in history as an herb of purification.

All you have to do is light the smudge stick and allow it to smoke. Wafting the smoke around your entire body, especially around the crown of the head, the heart, the palms and the soles of the feet is a good pattern for smudging. In addition to smudging your physical body before the ritual, it is also common to have a bowl of saltwater on your workspace or altar that you can dip your hands in for purification. You will be working with your hands and holding your Magickal tools and so clean hands are a must.

Purification Of The Space
Purifying the space is similar to purifying the self. Wherever you are working, you want to make sure that your area is free of any unwanted energies and that you are discharging and letting go of anything

that will disrupt or interfere with your ritual. The energy of your space needs to be relieved of stagnant energies and prepared for sacred rites.

Smudging is a powerful way to do this and you can go directly from smudging yourself to smudging the area where you will be working. I also like to place a lot of candles around the room or area and light them at this time. Fire is very cleansing and purifying and it sets the tone for what's to come.

You may find other Wiccan paths that have more specific ways of purifying and cleansing the ritual space before casting a circle. But these have been my tried and true methods for many years and are a common means of simple purification.

Creation Of The Sacred Space
The creation of the sacred space is what you do to open up the reality of Magick in front of or near an altar. Setting up your altar space will usually occur before you have cast your circle of Magick. By doing

this you are creating a sacred space for rituals. Once the circle is cast, I don't want to leave it.

Your altar will contain your sacred ritual tools and any other ingredients you care to bring to the table as offerings to your chosen deities. You may also want to have some elaborate decorations and include some other tools for any spell work you have planned during this casting. As you are preparing your altar for Magick you are creating a sacred space to hold your Magick.

Once the altar is prepared, you can begin the cast your circle of Magick. The circle is protection from outside influences and forces and it is also simply sacred energy that you create to announce your purpose and intentions. A circle will call upon the four cardinal directions and the four elements as you face each direction. Many circles cast are an average of 9ft wide, but if you are solitary, you may not need quite as much room. Also, even if you are in solitary practice, you can make your circle as wide as the room you are in. Trust your intuition and let it guide you.

Invocation Of The Deities

This next step is what arises after you have cast your circle and fully prepared your space for Magick and divine rite. You can now ask for the deities of your beliefs to come to your circle and work with you in your Magick. Invoking the deities is a simple and elegant gesture of gratitude to announce that you are prepared to honor them with your altar space and your Magick rituals.

I usually have a form of deity represented on my altar space with an offering of food and herbs, or flowers and wine. During my invocations, I will announce the deity or deities that they are welcome to partake of the offerings I have laid out for them. All you have to do to invoke the deities you are calling upon is to ask for their presence and to honor them with your thanks.

Some covens, circles, and solitaries will have more elaborate invocations and readings to call upon their chosen deities and that is perfectly normal. It really just depends on your chosen path and how you wish to practice this important part of the ritual.

Observing The Ritual

Observing the ritual is the actual action that you begin to take to engage with the purpose of your rite or ritual. This can mean a whole lot of things including the lighting of candles and incense, the use of altar tools including the athame, chalice, wand and pentacle, the casting of a spell, or the further honoring of a deity through sacred actions, feasting, drinking, and more.

Observing the ritual is the following through with the goals and actions laid out by your Book of Shadows. It is the recipe for the rites you have created or are using to perform a manifestation. It can take as little as ten minutes and as long as an hour or more. It truly depends on your Magickal purposes with each ritual and spell.

Raising The Energy

Raising the energy of the Magick ritual or spell means that you are bringing it to a head. After observing the rites, there needs to be a moment in the ritual in which you are deeply connected to the source of your power and your gift of connection to the Great Divine. The power within you is not the power you have created in your circle and as you raise this energy, you must feel it with your ritual as a way to honor the existence of power created.

Raising the energy could be a simple act of connection to your deities again and communicating with them. You may choose to hold your arms up above your head with your palms open toward the sky to bring this energy to the source powers that be. You can also guide the energy into a specific direction by clearly stating the results of observing your ritual. Making declarations about the power and Magick you have created in your ceremony will enhance it and reinforce it.

It is an important step so that you aren't just performing some actions and then closing your circle. You need to take time to be present with the energy created and the results of your ritual so that it can be fully released into the universe.

Grounding Your Power

Grounding your power comes after it has been raised. It is a sort of decompression after some intense spiritual awakening and awareness inside of your circle and during your potent Magickal ritual. Before you can return to the "real world" you have to ground your power and fully relax into your Magick invocations.

Grounding your power can be a lovely part of the celebration of your ritual. You can eat some of the food from your altar that you are sharing with your deities. Enjoying the feast you have laid out in honor of them is an honor to them as well and helps you ground your energy. You can also do a simple meditation while still in your circle that helps you reconnect with your energy after being so open and connected to Spirit.

All of the ways you ground your energy within your ritual will likely occur as a result of whatever your spell or ritual is. Not all rituals will involve food offerings, but it can be helpful to have a snack right afterward. Many beginning witches and Wiccans aren't fully aware of how much energy it takes to invoke Magick. Replenishing your energy after the ritual observations is a good way to take care of your inner Magick.

Ground your energy with a few words of thoughtfulness about your experience, or journal about it in your Book of Shadows.

Breaking The Circle With Gratitude

The final step to the Wiccan ritual is to break the circle and offer thanks. This step is vital to the creation of your Magick and the results of your ritual. Having a simple cord cutting with the space and experience will help you continue forward with your day or night without any attachments. It also helps the energy know where to go and that it is time to manifest outside of your circle.

To break your circle, you can simply rotate through the cardinal directions and thank each space and element for joining you on your journey and through your rituals. It is also a good time to give thanks to the God and the Goddess and to have gratitude for anything else that comes up.

Using and attitude of gratitude in all of your Magick is a very powerful portion of making Magick come to life. When you speak or think your words of thanks, you are creating that energy and informing the Great Divine that you are ready to invoke the Magick you just ritually performed.

Breaking the circle is the final motion to declare your honesty and honor with your path and your ritual. Leave the circle only once you have visited every direction like you did when you opened the circle and thanked the Goddess and the God.

These 8 ritual steps are a common way that many Wiccans will set up the rituals, rites, and spells. For some, they will be a lot less elaborate in a pinch or on the go. Once, while in an airport bathroom, I need to perform a ritual of protection. I had to quickly address each direction and create a moment of gratitude in a bathroom stall. But it still works no matter where you are. The point is that you are calling upon the powers that be to hear your call and listen to your Magick and the steps are the foundation of how to make that work well for you.

As you get better acquainted with your own ritual practices and spells, you can use these steps as a guidepost to help you organize what you are wanting to do. These are the best steps to create a sacred space and call upon the divine.

The next chapter will cover the Wheel of the Year and what each celebration represents. Sabbats and Esbats are one of the major reasons you will need these ritual steps and guidelines.

Chapter 5: Understanding The Wheel Of The Year

Wiccan celebrations, rites, and rituals are often connected to the sacred Wheel of the Year. It is the calendar year that is associated with the seasons and cycles of change that cyclically occur and help us travel through the reality of life, death, and rebirth every year. The story of the Wheel of the Year follows the relationship of the God and the Goddess and how they come together to create life in order to go through their own cycles of life, death, and rebirth.

You have already learned a little bit about this cycle from Chapter 2: The deities of the Moon and Sun. Now you can delve more deeply into the ritual practices of these times of celebration. The Wheel of the Year consists of 8 Sabbats which will be explained in detail, but first, let's start with the Esbats.

Esbats

Esbats are Moon rituals and celebrations. They take place once or twice a month typically and will often involve a coven ritual, circle gathering, or solitary honoring of the Moon. The Full Moon is the most common occasion for Esbat worship and celebration and it has become a very potent and powerful time for many people across the planet.

Even if you are a solitary and you are honoring the Moon on your own, think about how many Wiccans and witches in the world are doing the exact same thing. We are never alone on a Full Moon and that is something to remember. If you are not in a coven and you are on a solitary path, you can invite friends, even if they aren't practicing witches, into your circle of magic and show them how you like to honor the Moon.

It is a very sacred time of communication, opening, rebirth, and honesty with the self and others. Many Wiccans will have a "Full Moon in the nude party" or will celebrate with drinks and food, while others will hold more elaborate rituals and do serious spell work or consecrating ritual tools. It always depends on the Wiccan who is practicing.

I enjoy having a ritual ceremony on both the Full Moon and the Dark Moon before she becomes a New Maiden Moon. The Dark Moon is the moment when the Crone has died and is in her quiet moments before rebirth. There is no crescent visible and it is the sacred womb before new growth can occur. I use both Full Moon and Dark Moon Esbats to take stock of my personal Magick as well as through the ritual work with a coven.

Sabbats

The 8 celebrations of the Wheel of the Year are divided into Greater and Lesser Sabbats. Before the Bricket Wood Coven began to incorporate the

Lesser Sabbats, the Pagan holidays were just the 4 fire festivals that marked midway points between the seasons, or cross-quarter days. The Lesser Sabbats fall on the solstices and equinoxes and are referred to as the quarter days. Traditionally, Samhain is the New Year of the Wiccan calendar and marks the first Great Sabbat. It is the final harvest before the Crone time and it is the beginning of the circular cycle of life echoed in every person and in every holiday of the year.

Samhain

Halloween, Feast of the Dead, Night of the Ancestors, Blood Harvest, Last Harvest
October 31st through November 2nd

Samhain (sow-when) is often considered the most important of the Sabbats. It marks a time of preparation and paying respects to the deceased ancestors and loved ones who have come before and shown us the way. It is the time when the veil is thin between worlds and the departed can be invited to attend the rituals and celebrations of this time. Many Wiccans will decorate their homes and altars with pumpkins, gourds, apples, cinnamon, spices, candles, herbs and offerings to their ancestors. It marks the time of the last harvest of the Wheel of the Year and it welcomes the dark night of the soul when we must all go within and face the darkest times with our inner light. Traditionally, it is open to a lot of powerful magic because of the energy of the night being stronger and longer and is a good time for Crone Magick and for making preparations for winter transformations.

Winter Solstice

Yule, Midwinter

December 20th-23rd (depending on when Winter Solstice falls)

Winter Solstice is a joyful celebration to mark the rebirth of the God Sun who has gone through his own death during the Autumn months. Winter Solstice is the longest night of the year before the days begin to grow longer because of the new birth of the Sun and the shift of the Earth to welcome more light and the impending Spring. It is common to light many candles and get warm by the Yule log, traditionally decorated with holly and herbs. It is usually a time of great feasting and the burning of the yule log is often to set up to last the whole night long. Evergreens, hollies, mistletoe, and other winter greens and herbs decorate the altar and the house. It is considered a Lesser Sabbat.

Candlemas

Imbolc, St. Brigid's Day, Bride's Day
February 1st-2nd

This is usually seen as a festival of light. The winter is still present and the frosts are still hard on the icy earth, but the promise of Spring is beginning to emerge. This is a time when the Goddess is a young girl and the Celtic Goddess Brigid is often celebrated as the main female deity of this time. It has been considered a time of rededication to your craft and repledging of your devotion to your deities. It can also be a time to celebrate the Goddess preparing to meet the God for their Spring marriage and equality. Many candles are lit, typically white, and offerings to the Goddess are placed on the altar. It is a time to make devotions for the coming year.

Vernal Equinox

Ostara, Festival of Trees

March 20th-23rd (depends on the year and when the equinox falls)

The Spring Equinox marks the time when the night and the day are in perfect balance and when the Maiden Goddess and youthful Sun God are children of love and can come together to join each other. This is a time of fertility and new beginnings and is celebrated with the concept of eggs as represented by the Goddess Ostara. The myth of the Easter Bunny was actually taken from the deity Ostara who carries her eggs of fertility like seeds of abundance to be planted in the soil with the help of her rabbit consort, which some Wiccan circles see as a God form. The Green Man is also another form of the God at this time. Altars are decorated with colorful eggs, spring flowers, seeds, and other springtime abundance.

Beltane
May Day
May 1st

Beltane is another of the four Greater Sabbats and fire festivals which marks the midway point between Spring and Summer. A bonfire is a traditional part of the celebration as well as the act of dancing around the maypole. It is a fertility festival and symbolically interprets the consummation of the marriage between the Goddess and the God, as noted in the maypole dance and other symbolic sex rites. There are usually a lot of dances around the fire as well as drinks and delicious treats. Both men and women wear flowers in their hair and on their clothing. Altars are usually decorated with seasonal herbs, flowers, and fruits, as well as honey and oatcakes.

Summer Solstice

Litha, Midsummer Night, Midsummer
June 20th-23rd (depending on the calendar year and when it falls)

This is the point when the sun shines the longest in the sky and marks the height of the Sun's power. The God form is his fully formed and most virile and the celebration is a solar holiday. It is a time to celebrate the growing children of Mother Earth who represent her seeds planted in her soil womb. And as they grow with the power of the Sun God, the energy of light is a powerful force to open and prepare the growth of their offspring. This is the time of the Mother Goddess and altars are decorated to celebrate her fullness, along with the high light and brightness of the Sun God.

Lammas

Lughnasadh, The First Harvest, Festival of the First Fruits
August 1st-2nd

Lammas falls midway between the Summer Solstice and the Autumnal Equinox. It marks the moment of the first harvest when Mother Goddess can begin to give birth to her offspring. It is the first of three Autumn harvest celebrations and is celebrated by baking of bread to symbolizes the God and then eating it as part of the ritual. It is essentially a breaking of the bread to celebrate the fruits of the harvest. The grains and wheat to make bread are referred to as the "first fruits" of harvest and other foods are equally valuable to the altar and the Lammas celebration. Bonfires and candles are common for celebrations.

Autumnal Equinox

Mabon, The Second Harvest, Wine Harvest, The Fruit Harvest,

September 20th-23rd (depending on the calendar year and when it falls)

This is the second of three harvest festivals (the last being Samhain) and it is a time of thanksgiving and sharing the bounty of the harvest with others. Many foods will be stored for the winter months ahead and the festival marks another time of celebrating the offerings and abundance form the Goddess and the God for providing the offspring of their sacred union. Corn dollies are a common altar feature as well as other fruits and foods to celebrate the prosperity of the harvest. Many people will host elaborate and delicious feasts to consume the foods in gratitude. It is also a time for enjoying wine and celebrating the fruits of labor.

The Wheel of the Year is a modern Wiccan experience. The origins of these celebrations are pre-Christian, Celtic, and Germanic religions. It wasn't until the popularization of both the Greater and Lesser Sabbats by modern Wiccan culture that all were celebrated together throughout the course of the year. The traditional Wiccan practices work with the Wheel of the Year as the story between the Goddess and the God and their courtship, marriage, consummation and eventual birth and death, passing into the underworld before repeating the cycle anew.

Both the Goddess and God go through their own cycles of life, death, and rebirth and join each other on that path. The Esbats work in correlation with these cycles and are celebrated in conjunction with the Sabbats, or separately, depending on your path and practice. Each celebration marks a pinnacle moment in the cycles of life that we all go through and it is an amazing and powerful way to be connected to the energy and nature of all rhythms and cycles.

These festivals and celebrations are of great importance to the Wiccan path and as you begin to enjoy these rituals in your own practice, you can begin to understand the power of these cycles in your own life. The next chapter will continue the story of Wicca and give you the code of ethics needed to practice Magick mindfully.

Chapter 6:
The Wiccan Rede And The Rule Of Three

Your journey with Wicca is established when you accept that there are certain codes and ethics that must be embraced in order to work with this positive and affirming religion. There are many different takes on the following Wiccan standards and all Witches will believe what they will in order to perform the Magick of their path, however, if you are interested in performing Magick the Wiccan way than you must know the Wiccan Rede and the Rule of Three.

The Wiccan Rede

The Wiccan Rede is a principle of performing Magick that essentially states that you will agree not to hurt anyone in the process. You can find your way forward more easily and more fluidly if you are working in harmony with others and not in opposition. There are certainly those who practice

Magick that is intended to cause harm to a specific individual or group, and as you will find out in the next section about the Rule of Three, there is a good reason to avoid vindictive or negative casting in the direction of another.

Wicca is all about affirming life and comes from the positive stance of worshipping and appreciating all of the beings in nature. It is a respect for the power each of us carries and that we have the responsibility to respect others and be clear about our own personal motives when we cast Magick.

Often times, Wiccans and witches will close their rituals, spells, and circles by stating something like, "for the good of all", or "harming no other." When you are at that final step of the ritual, step number 8, you can announce something of this nature to clearly state your intentions to do no harm to others in your Magick.

The original wording of the Wiccan Rede, "an it harm none, do what ye will," is a little old-fashioned for many modern witches. This original statement is documented by Doreen Valiente who was a part of the original Gardnerian Wiccan coven, Bricket Wood and was responsible for writing many of the coven's publications. The Old English format ("an" meaning "if", and "ye" meaning "you") was part of that coven's choice of declaration and it can, of course, be changed to anything else that resonates with the modern witch. I usually say something along the lines of, "for the benefit of all and with no ill will..."

The Wiccan Rede essentially means this: if you aren't harming anyone you can do whatever you want! It is thought that this Rede was potentially inspired by Aleister Crowley, the famous occultist, from his own religion which stated, "Do what thou wilt shall be the whole of the Law." Aleister Crowley had made a big impression on Gardner and his coven and they even shared a friendship.

A longer version of the Rede was created sometime after the popularization and dissemination of Wiccan practices. A long poem in an American Pagan Magazine titled, "Rede of the Wiccae" was the demonstration of an even deeper perspective of the law of harming none and it goes like this:

The Long Rede/ Rede Of The Wiccae

"Bide within the Law you must, in perfect Love and perfect Trust.
Live you must and let to live, fairly take and fairly give.

For tread the Circle thrice about to keep unwelcome spirits out.
To bind the spell well every time, let the spell be said in rhyme.

Light of eye and soft of touch, speak you little, listen much.

Honor the Old Ones in deed and name,
let love and light be our guides again.

Deosil go by the waxing moon, chanting out the joyful tune.
Widdershins go when the moon doth wane,
and the werewolf howls by the dread wolfsbane.

When the Lady's moon is new, kiss the hand to Her times two.
When the moon rides at Her peak then your heart's desire seek.

Heed the North winds mighty gale, lock the door and trim the sail.
When the Wind blows from the East, expect the new and set the feast.

When the wind comes from the South, love will kiss you on the mouth.
When the wind whispers from the West, all hearts will find peace and rest.

Nine woods in the Cauldron go, burn them fast and burn them slow.

Birch in the fire goes to represent what the Lady knows.

Oak in the forest towers with might, in the fire it brings the God's
insight.   Rowan is a tree of power causing life and Magick to flower.

Willows at the waterside stand ready to help us to the Summerland.

Hawthorn is burned to purify and to draw faerie to your eye.

Hazel-the tree of wisdom and learning adds its strength to the bright fire burning.

White are the flowers of Apple tree that brings us fruits of fertility.

Grapes grow upon the vine giving us both joy and wine.

Fir does mark the evergreen to represent immortality seen.

Elder is the Lady's tree burn it not or cursed you'll be.

Four times the Major Sabbats mark in the light and in the dark.

As the old year starts to wane the new begins, it's now Samhain.

When the time for Imbolc shows watch for flowers through the snows.

When the wheel begins to turn soon the Beltane fires will burn.

As the wheel turns to Lamas night power is brought to Magick rite.

Four times the Minor Sabbats fall use the Sun to mark them all.

When the wheel has turned to Yule light the log the
Horned One rules.

In the spring, when night equals day time for
Ostara to come our way.
When the Sun has reached it's height time for Oak
and Holly to fight.

Harvesting comes to one and all when the Autumn
Equinox does fall.
Heed the flower, bush, and tree by the Lady blessed
you'll be.

Where the rippling waters go cast a stone, the
truth you'll know.
When you have and hold a need, harken not to
others' greed.

With a fool no season spend or be counted as his
friend.
Merry Meet and Merry Part bright the cheeks and
warm the heart.

Mind the Three-fold Laws you should three times bad and three times good.

When misfortune is enow wear the star upon your brow.

Be true in love this you must do unless your love is false to you.

These Eight words the Rede fulfill:
"An Ye Harm None, Do What Ye Will"

According to the story of this poem, the New England witch who wrote it named Adriana Porter claimed to have been practicing the craft years before Gardner began to introduce Wicca to the public. Many others believe that it was actually written in the 1960s and there has been no official evidence to determine the true history.

The Long Rede has since been incorporated into many Wiccan traditions and contains several statements about how to perform rituals and cast a circle, what the sacred trees represent, the phases of the moon, the wind directions and what they mean, as well as reference to the Sabbats. The entire poem is essentially the condensed Wiccan practice in one rhyming text. If the whole poem is too much in the beginning, the final two lines will suffice to get the message across in your craft:

These Eight words the Rede fulfill:
"An Ye Harm None, Do What Ye Will"

The interpretation of either the short or long Rede is to understand it as good counsel and advice. The word "rede" actually means "counsel" and so it is not necessary to think of it as a firm law or demand. Wicca has no central authority figure or even authoritative outlook and so the Rede has been established in Wiccan culture as being good words to live by.

You can suggest it as a way to keep you in balance with your practice and as a general rule of thumb for any Magick you perform. It is well worth it when you consider the next advice from the Wiccan point of view.

The Rule Of Three

Also known as the "Law of Three" or the "Threefold Law", this concept is a part of several Wiccan traditions. Not all paths choose to incorporate this rule, and you can determine in your solitary practice if it is important to your craft. I prefer it myself and after decades of practicing witchcraft, I can say from my own experiences that things seem to manifest in threes, or by the law of three anyway, no matter what you choose to believe.

The Rule of Three essentially states that every act of Magick that is performed in ritual, spell, or intention will return to you threefold, whether it is a negative or a positive intention. It has a lot of relationship to the laws and ideas of karma that have been established in many Eastern religious practices and in fact, many modern witches and Wiccans have adopted the rules of karma into their practices as a complement to the Rule of Three.

The interpretation of the number three is different for practitioners and as some will see "three times" meaning three separate occasions of return on your spell, others will see it as amplification or enhancement, like it is being multiplied in energy. It can honestly show up either way and it is just not something we have control over when it comes. The universe works in mysteries ways.

Origins of the Rule of Three are difficult to pinpoint but generally, it is considered the addition of Gerald Gardner and his coven. It wasn't considered to be a part of his original Wiccan teachings but the Rule of Three was cited in his stories of fiction about the craft. Initiates of Gardnerian Wicca took the concept of the Law of Three and instituted it into new covens as it spread across to Australia and North America, making it a more common part of the Wiccan culture.

The Rule of three, although not adopted by all Wiccan practitioners is explained in other ways by using the Law of Cause and Effect or the Law of

Return, each of which basically states that what you put out comes back to you. If you cast negative Magick or choose to cause harm to another, you will likely receive the same in return. While if you are seeking to harm none and working with positive and affirming energy, you will receive that in return instead.

Your choices with the rules are up to you and as they basically state together as a unit, your best bet with Magick is to treat it responsibly and with respect. It is not to be toyed with for the sake of yourself and the sake of others. The energy of Magick should be used with good intention and with the honesty and understanding that what you put out comes back to you, by the power of three or not.

Continuing into the next chapter you will learn how to apply all of the knowledge you have gained so far, plus a little extra, to discover the steps of casting a circle of Magick and setting up your altar. It is the bread and butter of crafting and will set you up to start creating your own spells and rituals today!

Chapter 7:
How To Cast A Magick Circle And Set Up Your Wiccan Altar

The Wiccan beliefs are all connected to the origins of Pagan rituals and witchcraft. Many of the rituals and castings come from ancient notions and concepts of how Magick is created and the casting of the circle and setting of the altarpieces is no different. The practice of engaging with this part of your Magick practice is where you will usually always begin. This is the foundation of your house of Magick and as you get better acquainted with your purpose and intentions, your altar will evolve with you and your circle will show up for you every time.

There are so many different ways that Wiccans will perform these steps and after several years of working with many different paths, practices, people, and on my own, I have distilled the basics down to a simple set of steps to help you get your footing with these magic principles.

You will need some equipment and tools and a lot of it you probably have lying around the house or being used for other things. A rule of thumb if you are gathering items for your rituals and spells from your kitchen or other household items: purify your tools ahead of time. You may recall from the chapter on rituals and preparations that it is important to purify yourself and your space before beginning a ritual. The same is true of objects and tools that you will use, especially if they have never been used for Magick before or are regularly used and need to be purified before another use.

There are a lot of different options for what you can use and in Chapter 10 I will go into greater detail about the Wiccan tools and what each one is used for. For now, your focus can be on casting the circle and preparing your altar. You also can cast a circle without any objects or tools at all and as you get familiar with the practice, you will understand what I mean.

The Circle

A Magick circle is a sacred space. It is the way that all witches begin their journey of connection to their sacred energy and the energy of Spirit. The circle represents many things symbolically and historically. A circle is a ring that has no beginning or end and is eternal, constantly flowing and direct in its force. A circle, or ring, is also a symbol of sacred union.

In the craft, the Magick circle is your source of protection and the place where you contain all of the energy of your Magick. It is the home you create for yourself while you cast and as you work with the energy available from within the circle of energy, power, and protection. The sacred reality of any circle you cast is that it is an invisible realm of sanctity and blessing that is a powerful shield to unwanted influences. It holds you in and keeps other things out, or vice versa depending on the Magick you are conjuring.

The reason you need a Magick circle is for all of the reasons above. It is what will help you operate within your craft and hold you responsible for the energy you are creating. It is the sacred space where you are able to invoke the God and Goddess as well and so it is an opening and a doorway to the great beyond. A Magick circle is simple or elaborate and feels energetically protective and light. As you get better acquainted with how energy works, you will know when your circle is fully formed because you will just feel it. It aligns you with your inner Magick as you present your craft to the outer world.

There are several techniques for casting a circle in Wicca and it will be different for a lot of people. In covens, there will be specific ways that you will cast your circle depending on the practices of that coven. For the solitary or eclectic practitioner, it will be very unique to your own style of rituals and Magick.

Some witches will use nothing in the way of tools or ritual elements to mark their circle. They will simply face each direction and point a finger of power to call upon the directions and the elements. This can actually create a very powerful circle and it is especially useful if you need to cast one and you are out somewhere without any of your tools or need to be discreet. The simple act of walking the circle, or using your finger to point it out as you call upon the directions is simple, easy and effective.

Another way to do it is to mark the four corners, or quarters, of the circle with each of the four elements. You can use a representation of each element in its simplest form. For example, you could place a dish of salt or soil in the North to represent Earth energy, a feather or a smoking incense stick in the East to represent Air, a candle in the South to represent Fire, and a dish or chalice of water in the West to represent Water.

As you invoke the elements in your circle you can set each item in the proper direction to build the circle physically. Some will also just place the elements on the altar and use a wand or athame to point out the energy of the circle. For those working in covens, the bodies of the members are what form the edges of the circle, either in a seated or standing position.

Other tools that are used to represent the corners and the elements are the traditional altar tools that you will learn a lot more about in Chapter 10, but for the sake of understanding the circle, you can learn about what each tool represents in the casting of the circle. The Pentacle is the symbol for the North, feathers or a sword (athame) can be used to call upon the East, a wand can be used for the South, as well as a lit candle, and the Chalice is the tool of the West to represent water and the sacred feminine.

Each of these tools may be used differently according to whatever brand of Wicca you are choosing to practice, for example, some will use the wand in the East and the athame in the South. You will be able to choose according to your own practice and preferences. After all, Wicca is a creative art and ritual practice and sometimes it is okay to just go with the flow and let yourself intuitively decide while you are setting up your circle and your altar.

In Wicca, the circle of Magick is used to prepare you for the rites, spells, and invocations to practice your identity as a witch and a Wiccan. It is a special time to devote yourself to your deities and create space for the sacred offering and ceremony. It means a lot that you give yourself the opportunity to come up with the circle Magick that works best for you and you can eclectically choose from a lot of different Wiccan paths, or even invent your own until you decide on one that will resonate with your Wiccan needs and path.

How To Cast A Circle – Step By Step

For these instructions, I will use come of the traditional Wiccan altar tools and offer notes and suggestions for alternatives. You can choose to cast your circle with nothing more than your finger or a wand, but in these steps, I will teach you how to cast with the elements represented at each corner of your circle.

You will need the following items:

- Pentacle (Pentagram star or another symbol of Earth)
- Feathers
- Candle
- Chalice with water
- Smudge stick (preferably white sage)
- Lighter/matches

1. Light the smudge stick and purify yourself with the smoke, followed by the area where you will be casting your circle.

2. Decide how big you want your circle to be (it needs to be big enough for you to sit, stand, or work in) and be sure to purify this area well with sacred smoke.

3. Begin to cast your circle by calling upon the East position. (NOTE: If you need a compass to help you organize your circle, that's okay. It's best to figure it out ahead of time) To call upon the East, hold the feather or feathers out toward the East and say the following words or something similar:

    "Sacred East, Sacred Air, I call upon thee to my circle aware."

4. Place the feather(s) in the eastern part of the circle and move clockwise to the South

position. (NOTE: you can substitute the smoking smudge stick or another form of incense to represent Air and East)

5. Light the candle and hold it in your hand as you say the following words or something similar:

"Sacred South, Sacred Fire, I call upon thee with desire."

6. Place the candle in the position of the South. Be sure that it is stable in a candle holder before moving clockwise to the West. (NOTE: You can also use a wand, or other Wiccans will use an athame in the South position in addition to, or instead of, a candle)

7. Hold your chalice in hand and say the following words or something similar as you face the West:

"Sacred West, Sacred Water, I call upon thee, Mother, Father."

8. Place the chalice of water in the position of the West and then turn clockwise to face the North. (NOTE: If you don't have a chalice specifically for rituals, you can use a cup, bowl or dish of water in place of the chalice.

9. In the North facing position, hold the pentacle or other symbol and recite the following words or something similar before placing it in the North position:

    "Sacred North, Sacred Earth, I call upon thee for this rebirth."

10. Lay the pentacle in the North. (NOTE: You can replace the pentacle with a dish of salt or soil to represent the earthly North energy)

11. This is now the point in the circle casting when you call upon the fifth element of spirit. You can point your wand or finger, or simply hold your palms out and face up to call upon the God and Goddess to come into your circle to represent Spirit or any other form of a deity you prefer to practice with.

"Sacred Mother, Sacred Father, I call upon thee with my heart,
To cast this circle, and so it is right. Let us begin our sacred rite."

12. The circle is cast and you can begin your Magick! This might also be a good time to communicate that you intend to harm none before proceeding with any rituals or spell work.

A Note on Wording: You certainly don't have to rhyme and you can take these general offerings of how to call upon each corner and change them to your liking. I change what I say regularly as it pertains to the spells or rituals I am working on when I cast. It is certainly okay to address each circle according to what your Magick of today is and it is a creative process all around. Play with the wording and have fun! Who knows, you might have an inner poet waiting to come out and cast Magick.

This is the very basic step-by-step guide to casting a circle. As you practice, you will intuitively draw up new ways of casting as they feel appropriate. In general, it is a good practice to acknowledge each direction by facing it and saying a few words of invocation and to finalize the circle by inviting in the spiritual energies that will be present with your work.

When you close your circle, it is beneficial to go back through the same steps from the position you started in and going back around with an expression of gratitude for the energies and elements that provide you with the energy and protection you needed to perform Magick and ritual. You can use words like the following to help you close your circle:

"Thank you to the blessed Air and East, thank you for your presence in my circle. And so it is.

Thank you to the blessed Fire and South, thank you for your presence in my circle. So mote it be.

Thank you to the blessed Water and West, thank you for your presence in my circle. And so it is.

Thank you blessed Earth and North, thank you for your presence in my circle. So mote it be.

Thank you Goddess and thank you God for your sacred gift of Magick divine. And so it is.

These Eight words the Rede fulfill:
"An Ye Harm None, Do What Ye Will"

The closing of the circle can be more elaborate if you wish and for beginners, sometimes simple is the best. As you grow in your practice you will come up with all of the right ways that you want to open and close your circle. The key take-away when doing both is that you offer your thanks for the Magick you have made and for the presence of the Great Divine in your craft.

The Wiccan Altar is another sacred space where you can call upon the divine energies to help you cast your Magick and perform your rituals. If you prefer to keep all of your objects and Magick tools on the altar space, rather than in the position of the four corners, then you can just mark your circle with your wand or finger and then organize all of the other items at the altar space.

The Altar

The Wiccan Altar is the sacred space where you are able to place your offerings to the God and Goddess and perform your Magickal work. It is almost like your workshop if you were a tinkerer or a carpenter. The placement of your altar tools relates to the power of the four corners and the elements involved. It is a very sacred act to layout these offerings, gifts and sacred implements and so it should be in a part of your house where you can keep it safe and undisturbed by others. If you live in a household of Magick with others who respect your practice, then you will likely be able to display it in more open and obvious places.

The Wiccan Altar is usually where you will find the representations of the Goddess and God or other deity forms. Statues and figures of each are sometimes displayed, and some of the altar tools are also representative of the Goddess of the God as you will continue to learn about in later chapters.

Throughout the Wheel of the Year, the Sabbats and Esbats, the altar is the presentation piece for your devotions to the Lord and Lady or whichever deity form you prefer to worship. With each season there will be a variety of different objects and offerings to place on the altar. As you read in Chapter 5, each season will boast a different type of altar decoration according to what is growing and being harvested at the time.

Spring flowers, seeds, and colorful eggs are a good choice for the Ostara celebrations (Spring Equinox) while pumpkins, gourds, apples, and corn dollies are more prevalent at the Samhain altar. Each celebration throughout the year will inform you of exactly how to decorate your altar and for the most part, when you are celebrating a Sabbat or an Esbat, it can display your altar tools, and your representations of your deities, as well as any other Magick you are conjuring in the moment.

Some Wiccans who are new to this path have asked me if you even need to have an altar and the truth is, you don't. An altar is symbolic of what you are seeking to worship and what kind of intentions and Magickal purposes you have, but it is certainly not required to honor your deities and cast a circle to perform a ritual. Your Magick comes from within and will be honored and received, altar or no. Basically, you can be the altar.

Historically, altars have been around for as long as people have been looking at the stars and painting images on caves. It is a completely natural urge to build an altar and you don't have to choose to follow the specific steps I have outlined for you when you are setting up your altar. These steps are just a Wiccan guideline to help get you started but you might find that as you are getting going with your practice, you may want to simplify how it is set up.

Sometimes all an altar has to be is a place with a candle and some spoken intentions. An altar can be made anywhere you are in fact. I happen to keep a travel altar with me with small and simple objects, in case I am traveling and I need to cast some Magick. It is worth it to consider that your altar is an extension of your practice and therefore an extension of YOU, so while you are going through the steps to setting up your altar, keep that in mind.

How To Set Up A Wiccan Altar – Step By Step

The steps to setting up your altar are as easy as casting a circle. You don't have to cast a circle before you set up your altar, in fact, I usually set mine up before I begin any casting and ritual. The first thing to consider before you create your altar space is to determine if it is an everyday ritual altar that you need for regular use, or if you are setting it up for a particular Sabbat.

I will usually keep an everyday altar set up with all of my tools and implements ready to use so that they are held in a sacred space until use. You can choose to arrange your altars only when you need them for rituals as well.

The following steps will provide you with the guidance you need to set up a ritual altar to use in a variety of spells. I will be using the traditional Wicca in celebration of the Goddess and God and you can modify it to your needs and tastes. Many altars will usually face or be placed in the North or the East, but you can actually set up your altar in whatever corner is befitting your Magick.

You will need the following items:

- Candle (at least one, but more if desired)
- Feathers
- Incense or smudge stick
- Chalice with water (or wine)
- Cauldron or ritual bowl (fireproof or fire safe is ideal)
- Pentacle or pentagram
- Athame
- Wand
- Dish or bowl of salt
- Seasonal fruits and other offerings like baked bread or oatcakes

- Images or objects of the deities, like statues or antlers

- Ritual cloth (optional)

1. Begin by laying out your ritual cloth if you desire using one. You don't have to but I think it adds a nice ceremonial touch. It can also protect surfaces from water, fire, and melting wax.

2. Determine which direction your altar will face or will be positioned in. I like to place mine in the direction of the North facing the South, and you can choose whatever feels most appropriate for your ritual needs.

3. Find the direction of the East and place your feathers and incense in that area. You can arrange the feathers so that they are standing up in a vase, or just lay them out on the table. This is also where you will place

your incense. Both the smoke and feathers represent the air element.

4. You can light the incense and say a few words of invocation to honor the air and the East like you saw in the steps for casting a circle.

5. Next place your candle in the South near your wand and athame. If you like to put either one of these in the direction of the East you can, but if you are just laying them out on the altar, they can go wherever you prefer them to be. I like to put my athame on one side of the candle and my wand on the other.

6. You can light the candle at this point, or wait until everything else has been set up and make your final action.

7. In the Western part of the altar space, you can place the chalice. I like to fill mine with sacred water I have collected from the sea,

waterfall, or river, but I will also fill it with ceremonial drink depending on what I am doing. An alternative, especially if you are planning to use the chalice for ritual drinking or symbolic union between the Goddess and God, then you can just have a bowl of water in the West and leave the chalice open for ritual uses. You can also place items from the sea or rivers, like seashells or river stones, that will add to the energy of water and the West.

8. In the North area of the altar space, you can set an image of the deities. I like to place an old-world replica of the Goddess called the Venus of Willendorf and next to her I will lay some stag antlers to represent the Horned God (male deity). You can get creative with how you want to arrange these items but they are good things to have centrally located on your altar.

9. Your pentacle can go in this area as well and you can place them next to each other or around one another however it feels the best. A dish of salt will be representative of the North and can be placed in this area or nearby. Anywhere will do, really.

10. I usually like to place my cauldron in front of my candle for easy access and ritual work, but you can find where it feels best for your work.

11. Set out any seasonal offerings like fruit, nuts, seeds, baked bread, etc.

12. Additionally, you can always place these items where they feel the best according to your intuition for whatever spell or ritual you are practicing.

13. Light the candle and open your circle once your altar is prepared.

An important item of note is that your presentation on your altar does not have to follow these steps verbatim. You can coordinate your altar however it looks and feels right to you. It is more about the energy of the elements that you are bringing to the table and how you are arranging them is your own work of art. You can look at YouTube videos and online tutorials to give you the satisfaction of seeing how other Wiccans and witches are organizing their altars, but I will strongly encourage you to enjoy the creativity of designing it on your own.

Your altar will transform and change regularly because you will be using it regularly. It is a living piece of spiritual art and devotion and so you want to make sure that it stays clean and well cared for. It can be something that you change around weekly or monthly or every time you use it for spell work.

My altar for spells and rituals is usually always in a state of flow. I will usually reorganize it at the end of a spell or ritual and set everything back to its resting state before I cast any more magic from this space. It is good to keep it organized and in a state of readiness so that there isn't any energetic congestion incorporated into your spells and rituals. You can also regularly smudge your altar to keep it purified.

The altar is a part of your Magick. It is an extension of yourself and your devotion to your craft and it can be a wonderfully artistic and creative experience so enjoy it! You don't have to know everything about altars to have one; you just have to have a safe place that feels sacred to you and a few items to symbolically represent your personal craft.

In the next chapter, we will take your practice further and start talking about what Magick really is, why it is different from the term "magic" and how it influences your craft. There will be explanations

for the different kinds of conditions of Magick and
how you are the one influencing it always.

Chapter 8:
Magick – The Science Of Understanding Oneself And One's Conditions

The Science of Magick is wisdom from the days of old and the term "science" is probably too confining when you are talking about the much bigger and broader concepts behind Magick. Science is only a subtle fraction of what Magick really is and for many new Wiccans and witches, there is a curiosity about where the word even comes from, why it is so often seen spelled with a "k" on the end of it, and what the definition really is.

This chapter is devoted to explaining what Magick is and what some of the techniques are that will show you your conditions with Magick and how to align yourself with it properly and respectfully.

The Meaning Of Magick

Magic is "the art of influencing events and producing marvels using hidden natural forces." This is the literal definition of magic. It is close participation with nature and working with co-creative energetic forces and transformations. Witches have long-known that in order to have what you want and need in this world you have to work with the energy of all things, not against it.

That is why in Wicca we see Magick as a co-creation, allowing none to believe that he or she has more power than anything else in the universe. We all have the power of Magick within and it is simply a question of knowing how to work with that energy and those unseen and mysterious forces. A witch will incorporate their own unique powers and energies into these forces in order to manifest magic. It is the power of that individual or coven that will co-create some magical intention.

You may have noticed that I have been spelling Magick with a "k" throughout this entire book. The reality is that you could spell it either way if you wanted. There isn't a rule in Wicca that says you have to spell it this way. The High Priestess who taught me in my early days was a devotee of Aleister Crowley and early Gardnerian Wicca. She had a fondness for this spelling because it was originated by Crowley in his own writings and teachings about occult Magick. That's really all it is and there isn't really a science to the word "Magick." It was just Crowley's way of differentiating his personal craft from any other concepts out there in the late 19th and early 20th centuries.

The History Of Magick

The rich and exciting history of Magick is far too dense to accurately describe in one book about beginning witchcraft, however it is important to realize that this world we live in has almost always had some form of Magick being practiced as long as humans have had the awareness to do it. There isn't really a date of origin for when people began to practice various forms of magic and yet there were early signs dating as far back as the Ancient Mesopotamians and Egyptians.

People have been performing rituals of consecration, banishment, conjuring, evocation, and healing since the dawn of civilization and it was only the fairly recent history of our evolution that Magick was seen as "evil" and was the subject of much controversy surrounding the age of witch hunts and Christian devotion.

Even still, what these Christian lords and bishops failed to admit was that everything they were doing was an equal act of Magick. Every part of a religious congressional ceremony is full of Magick practices and deals with connection to the unforeseen force known as "God", the male father deity of the Christian faith.

Prior to the Christian philosophy of Magick being evil, the acts of Magick that were performed were to help call the rains to get good crops or to protect a village from famine. In a way, Magick was a lot like a prayer to the celebrated deities of culture to make sure everything went smoothly in life.

Magick will always exist and in our modern culture, we are seeing it as an acceptable form of working with the self as well as personal spirituality in ways that allow a person to identify and enjoy their own personal power as well as the forces of nature. There are plenty of benefits to practicing Magick and the techniques are easy and simple for any beginning witch.

The Benefits And Techniques Of Magick

Magick is a benefit to anyone who has a need to go deeper into their own psyche, consciousness, and personal mysteries while at the same time, going more deeply into the mysteries of all life. It is an incredibly beneficial way for any person to exist because it requires a thoughtful and inquisitive look at the self and others, with a lack of judgment and a desire to work in harmony.

I have found through my own devotion to Wicca that I have learned how to be a much more compassionate and empathic person, as well as wiser and more thoughtful and mindful about everything I do. My life is rich and prosperous from within and I am able to look at myself very clearly because of how I live with Magick in my life.

In order to understand how Magick works and how to use it well, you really do have to know yourself. Another benefit of Magick is that it causes self-discovery and asks you to be deliberate and honest with all of your actions. This can be scary and unnerving for some at first, while it can be a totally liberating breath-of-fresh air for others.

Benefits aside, the techniques are how you will learn to explore Magick and what it can do to influence your life in positive ways. There are several I will list here that are some of the more common approaches, but remember that this is just a manual for beginners and as you go further on your path you will explore so many more ways to enjoy and practice Magick.

Banishing

The definition of banishing is to force to create and ending with something unwanted. Some Wiccans will use the term "exorcism" to describe banishing and the main idea is that you are trying to rid yourself of a presence of energy that is negative or unwanted.

Amazingly enough, you can use banishing spells in order to discharge unwanted energies while harming none and maintaining the Wiccan Rede. Banishing is not about hurting anyone or being mean. It is a Magickal act of declaring that you would like to release and let go of something that is not welcome in your life. It is an act of protection for yourself and others.

Sometimes, banishment can be seen as a way to improve your personal life by letting go of unwanted addictions or issues of low self-esteem. Banishing bad habits and negative thought patterns is just as much a part of Magick as banishing poltergeists is.

You can let go of a lot with a banishing technique and like with all of the witchcraft you learn on your journey, it is always about intention, how you word your intention, and your right actions to manifest that intention into reality.

Purification

Purification is another way to say "cleaning" or "clearing". Purification is the important step you must take before any ritual or rite that is being performed by either bathing or smudging yourself. The reason for purification is to clear and cleanse the body or any Magickal tools and any residue from former spells, or just a collection of energies that can disturb the pathways and channels of Magick.

Unlike banishment, purification is simply a metaphorical, symbolic, or literal washing away of impurities and energies that need to disperse and dissolve in order to create higher vibrational frequencies of energy. It is a very simple process as you have already read in the chapter about ritual preparations.

White sage, salt, and water are excellent tools of purification and several crystals and gemstones can be very purifying as well. It will benefit you to use Magickal purification methods prior to any spell or ritual and to regularly cleanse and clear your tools and Magickal implements.

Consecration

Consecration is an act of blessing something. Usually, this step will occur after the purification process and is what you do to imbue your sacred objects, self, and Magickal intentions with positive energy. Consecration is a lot like a ritual act and can actually be used as a method of performing rituals to consecrate certain things before using them in the rituals for devotions to God and Goddess.

I will often have rituals specifically devoted to caring for my altar tools by casting a circle on a waxing moon and having a ceremony to purify and consecrate them for future rituals. I will also perform a consecration during a ritual for something else, specific to a Sabbat or Esbat, or any other spell work. Consecration can be as simple as holding the tools or items in your hands and engaging your energy along with source energy to magically fill the object with sacred energy.

You can also use more elaborate rituals for consecration if desired. Some consecration methods involve charging items, or even your physical body under the sun or full moonlight. There are a lot of different methods and your personal intuition can help you determine your preferred method for consecration.

Invocation/Evocation

Invocation and evocation are sometimes used to mean separate things, while other Wiccans use these words interchangeably. Both words are defined as the act of invoking or evoking a response from a spirit or deity. Others will say that evocation means to call something out from within, suggesting that it is in relationship to your own inner wisdom and personal power, while invocation is related more to the higher dimensional beings we call deities.

Either way, both are a form of communication with higher wisdom and powers and calling upon them to be present in your journey with casting Magick. When I invoke my chosen deities, I speak to them directly and I present offerings of a certain kind in order to show them my respect. I will light candles and throw runes to read their responses and communication.

Evocation also means to elicit a response and when you are working to communicate with the Great Divine, you want to hear what it has to say. Some of my rituals are strictly about this type of communication and working with Spirit so that I can enhance my wisdom as I seek to grow and become more enlightened on my path. It is a condition of the craft that you are open to seeking higher levels of consciousness and both invocation and evocation are a doorway to that enlightened state.

Astral Travel

Astral travel is your own spiritual energy going away from your physical form to meet another dimensional reality. It is likely you have already astral traveled because many human beings will do this in their sleep without even realizing it or questioning it. It was just a dream, we think.

Astral travel is also sometimes referred to as astral projection. Your astral body is the spiritual format of your existence that has the capacity to move between worlds. A majority of people are not open to this type of work in an awakened state and it is something that comes with practice. It is a wonderful way to communicate with your higher self and the higher powers that be.

A Shaman I worked with many years ago asked me to go to the place of my original life. As a Wiccan, I believe in reincarnation and as the Shaman worked with me, she asked me to try and find the place of my first soul life on Earth. With her guidance and support, I was able to astral travel to a place and time that I had not known in this life and to see the origins of my first life as a soul.

It can be a scary experience if you are not accustomed to going on these inward journeys and quests and it will continually open up a lot of doors of understanding your own self and soul journey if you choose to practice astral travel. It has similarities to lucid dreaming which is a great way to start practicing this level of awareness.

Divination

Divination is a method of gaining understanding and awareness about all kinds of information. It is regarded as a way to "see" beyond the surface of things and deeper into the Collective Unconscious. Divination is a great way to go deeper into the mysteries of life and all of the ages from the past, present, and future.

It is often cited as being connected to your psychic awareness, clairvoyance, and vision-seeking capabilities. Astral travel and divination are often lumped together because your astral projection experiences are a form of divination in some cases. Other ways people will "divine" information is through channeling with spirit, scrying, tarot reading, and other similar methods.

It is a tool of Magick that will be very useful and helpful to your spell work and casting so that you can feel more connected to the correct path to help yourself and others. I use divination as a method of guiding other witches and Wiccans on their path by doing a celestial embodiment reading which allows me to divine what their soul blueprint is asking of them. Other diviners will use methods of this kind for similar purposes.

Divination can be used as part of your ritual connection to Spirit. As you practice your chosen path, the deities you communicate with will show you the way to understanding the universe as a whole and divination will be a tool of Magick that will help you understand your place in the Great Cosmic Dance.

With all of these techniques and benefits of Magick, you can extend your practice even further to other methods of opening and awakening. Many Wiccans will practice yoga as a tool of Magick in order to help them align more deeply with the energy of their chakras. Yoga is an Eastern philosophy that blossomed out of ancient Hindu religions. It is a way to practice wholeness and balance between all levels of self which can help you attain higher consciousness in all the Magick work that you do.

The Qabalah and the Eucharist have also been incorporated into some Wiccan and craft circles and so I will briefly mention them here as tools of understanding your personal Magick. The Qabalah is the Jewish Gnostic texts and some who practice the Alexandrian form of Wicca will also become acquainted with these teachings. The main symbol of this branch of spiritual wisdom is the Tree of Life which is interpreted as being the branches and levels of the different realities of life forms. These life forms include human beings, angles, gods, celestials and more. It demonstrates how we are interwoven and linked. The symbol can be seen sometimes in Magickal craftwork.

The Eucharist is often associated with the Christian Church as the breaking of bread and drinking of wine to commemorate the Last Supper. In Wicca, we use the Eucharist in our Magickal ceremonies to honor our deities and our own bodies.

These additional concepts are just the beginning of the rabbit hole you can explore that is "Magick". Going down one rabbit hole will usually lead to five more and so the adventure you take with Magick begins with these simple tools and techniques to get you started.

Moving forward into the next chapter, you will learn more about how to cast Magick spells. Many spells include a lot of the Magick techniques that you learned in this chapter, and you can also keep it simple and use your intuition. I find that the best way to cast spells is from the heart.

Chapter 9:
How To Cast Magickal Spells

Casting spells is one of my favorite parts of being a Wiccan and a witch. I deeply enjoy the creativity of conjuring, brewing and concocting and really when you get down to it, it is like a carefully designed elaborate dish that a chef might serve in a five-star Michelin restaurant. Spells are elegant and exquisite in every lighting of the candle and every herb bundle sacredly burned. It is a gorgeous act and it is a powerful aspect of your path with Wicca.

So what are spells, anyway? Basically, a spell is a recipe, action or procedure. It is something that is used through steps to help you shift, change, and transform energy so that you can manifest your intentions. It can change your own inner world to help you become better equipped to receive what you are asking for, and it can direct and conduct energy to be drawn to you, clearing the pathways and channels to find you.

Spells are great for so many different occasions and needs. They can be for a variety of purposes as well. Many people will say never to cast spells on certain days or nights of the year, or to avoid casting if you are under the weather, or have just had a string of bad luck. But the truth is, if your intentions are positive and you are working towards an important goal, there really isn't a time when you *shouldn't* cast a spell. The only time I would say not to is if you are not clear about your intentions. But more on that later on.

There are several different types of spells and as you go on your journey you will find endless resources to help you determine which spells align the most with your practice. There are so many different ways to perform any spell and as any witch will tell you a majority of the ones they are practicing are of their own invention. There are a lot of basics that we will cover that are relatively common to most spells you will cast. Here is a simple list of some of the different types of spells you might want to cast:

- Enchantments
- Charms
- Potions
- Poppets
- Love and Sex
- Prosperity, Wealth & Abundance
- Luck & Money
- Banishing
- Protection
- Purification
- Health & Well-Being
- Success & Career
- Moon and Sun
- Goddess and God
- Fertility
- Clairvoyance & Psychic Awareness
- New Beginnings & Endings

- And more

If you know the basic principles for casting a spell, you can take any one of these possible spell ideas and conjure your own Magick with it. The basics of spell casting are simple and are the foundation for any well-structured spell. With these simple steps, you will be able to create all of your own spells with a little research and a good amount of time.

The Five Basic Steps Of Spell Casting

Step 1: Prepare

Preparing for your spell is everything you do to make sure that you have what you need and that your intentions are clear. It's like going to the grocery store and buying everything you need to bake a cake, bringing it home, setting it all out on the counter and then concocting the recipe.

It is especially important during the preparation phase that you are very clear about what your spell is about and why you are doing it in the first place.

Clear intentions make for much bigger, better results. A spell can be very personal or for someone else and if you are casting on someone else's behalf, make sure you have their permission first.

Try to be as specific as possible. Ambiguous spells won't carry very far so try to avoid a spell to generally make your life better, or wishing for something like love without being clear about what kind of love, characteristics, qualities, etc. Specifics matter.

In the preparation phase, you can also work out what you want to say. Words carry a lot of meaning and give a lot of direction to what you are manifesting. Try to keep the words focused and concise. If you are getting too wordy in your rough drafts, edit it to have a clear and direct voice and intention. You will also want to steer clear of negative words that might be confusing to the energy you are trying to work with. Say "can", "will", "do", and avoid words like "won't", "can't", and "not".

As you are creating your spell, break it down into steps like you are writing a recipe to bake that cake. Designing your spell ahead of time makes it much clearer and more direct so that by the time you cast your circle you will be very ready to just proceed with the steps required to manifest your Magick.

If you have a really big goal that is going to take a lot of energy, you might also consider breaking your spell down into smaller, more achievable goals. For example, if your spell revolves around your career and your work life and you are aiming for a big promotion in your field, then start with what you need to work on first and make a spell for that, followed by the next ladder rung to climb. It helps the energy work with sustaining your overall purpose with you.

Your spell can be written down, revised, edited and reworked until it feels right. The preparation stage is all about planning and so this is when you can scribble it out on scratch paper to get it right. You certainly don't have to memorize it; that's what your book of spells is for. Once your spell has a working final draft, you can add it to your Book of Shadows for regular use.

Make sure you know the best timing to work the spell (day, night, Full Moon, etc.). You also want it to be at a time when you will be undisturbed by other people unless they are participating. Get your supplies and materials together and make sure you have everything you want for your spell on hand before you commit to doing it.

When you are getting ready before the moments of casting your spell, cleanse the space and make sure all of your tools, ingredients, and supplies are set up and ready for use, like a chef preparing to make an amazing meal. Make sure you will not be distracted by outside forces (including your cell phone- in fact, I would just turn it off).

Prior to the spell, you may want to do some special things for yourself like fasting or eating light so that your body is energetically unburdened and fully open to the process. You may also want to drink plenty of water, or do some kind of ritual bath or purification.

Step 2: State Of Mind

Your state of mind matters. Thoughts are energy and if you are thinking negatively, like worrying about if it will work or not or having anxiety that you aren't doing it the right way, then you will have a negative impact on the quality of your spell's output.

A healthy mindset is not hard to achieve with regular practice and an attitude of mental agility and toughness. Mindfulness and meditation practices are incredibly helpful and beneficial and can be used daily leading up to your spell, to keep your thoughts in a good balance.

The state of mind you want to attain during a spell is the place where your intuition works the best and where you can channel your power and spell work the most easily. An Alpha mind state refers to the length and rhythm of your brain waves. Your mind achieves an alpha state when you are able to meditate easily and let go of your worries and outside influences.

Your energy needs to have a relaxed quality so your state of mind can be pure to conduct Magick. If this seems challenging to you at first, I would recommend beginning daily meditation and mental focus practices to achieve a relaxed and free form state of mind. Positive thoughts are key to manifesting the Magick you want to create.

Step 3: The Intention Is Linked

The main purpose of your spell is declaring your intention and making it a reality and there are a few simple ways you can achieve this. You can use one, or all of these possible methods for making your intentions clear. And it is always up to you and your personal practice and the way you prefer to perform Magick.

You can simply state your intention clearly. You may have already written it down in the preparation phase and can now read it from a piece of paper that you wrote it on or declare it from memory. It is a good way to bring it out into the open, by speaking it aloud.

Use anything that stimulates your senses and forms a link or connection to your intention. I like to use green colored velvet in my money spells because the material reminds me of luxury and the color reminds me of cash money. Someone else might want to use a silver or cold cloth instead of green.

It's also good to find the aromas, flavors, colors, and anything else that is sensory that will help you invoke the intention you are working with.

Picturing the goal or intention in your mind is a powerfully effective tool. Creative visualization is something that really helps you manifest. If you can picture it in your mind then it can be a reality.

Other types of imagery or symbols can be useful as well. You can use Celtic symbols, runes, pictures, hieroglyphs, pieces of artwork, and so forth that will help you conjure the Magick you are looking for. You can draw or write these symbols or imagery on your altar space, carve them into candles, etc.

Objects can be helpful for linking intentions and can be kept on the altar or on your person to act as a reminder. Poppets are dolls that are usually constructed during spell work that can represent you or someone else to help with the intention. Jewelry, relics, artifacts, anything that has meaning to your goal can be used in your spell to help the intentions and goals become clearer.

Step 4: Raise, Direct, And Release The Energy

This step is all about how to give energy to the intention. Once your intention is clear, you can raise, direct and release the energy of your intention so that it is cast into the energy of all things, like a fishing line cast out to catch your desires and dreams.

Raising your energy comes from two places: internal and external sources. The internal source is your state of mind, the energy of your thoughts and desires, your wants and needs, and your emotional state. This is why it gets so important to have a clear and positive state of mind while you are casting your Magick. External sources are all of the things outside of you that you are co-creating Magick with. This will be your tools and ingredients, herbs, candles, deities, celestial bodies like the Sun and

Moon, astrological readings and symbols, runes, and so forth.

Keep in mind that as you are raising your energy there will be both sides of source energy at play and this is a very powerful feeling. For beginners, it can take some time to feel the energy being directed through yourself and your tools, but the more you practice the better you get at knowing how it feels.

It can take as little as five minutes to do this, or several hours and it all depends on what kind of spell you are doing, how elaborate it is, how many people are involved, etc. Some of the ways you can raise the energy of your intention are through creative visualization, rocking, drumming, chanting, singing, dancing, and even sexual arousal (sex Magick is a whole other rabbit hole).

Once you have reached a point where you feel like the raising of energy has reached its climax, you can begin to direct and release it. "Direction" is just maintaining focus on the intention. When you get lost in a trance state during the raising of the energy, coming back to your focused intentions is what directing the energy means.

Every witch has a different method for release and it can be a method you use every time, like a stomping or shouting release at the end, or a boom bang on a drum. You can ring a bell to signal the release of the energy, or state some clear and direct words. Burning something is a great way to release the energy as well as breaking something, like glass under a handkerchief. You can drink a concoction if you made one during your spell and that will signify the release, as will declaring "So mote it be!"

After you release the energy you should take a few minutes to ground your energy. You can do this with creative visualization by imagining any excess energy flowing down a river in your mind and into the cosmos, or flowing deep into the roots under the earth.

Step 5: Creating Channels

This step, the final one of casting spells, is how you help your spell work its way into the reality of your life. Creating a channel is all about creating openings for your intentions to become manifested. It is how you put yourself in the position to receive what you have asked for.

This can mean that if you cast a spell to meet your one true love, then after you have conjured your Magick, you might then start putting yourself out there by trying some online dating or going out more with friends to meet potential partners. It could mean going out for your own pleasure and doing the things that you love the most and seeing who shows up in these places.

Creating channels of opening helps then intention of your spell work well for you. You have to show up for the Magick. You can't just sit around and expect it to fall in your lap in the comfort of your living room. It is a way for you to show up for yourself and the Magick that you cast.

These simple steps are really all you need to know to build and create any spell from the ground up. Having the right framework makes all the difference and if you want to find a good way to make more out of your spells, the next chapter will talk about the traditional Wiccan tools that are regularly used in craftwork.

Chapter 10: Traditional Wiccan Tools Explained

The traditional tools of Wicca are also the traditional tools of many Pagan and occult arts and are frequently used by many witches and others who are not practicing Wiccans. We Wiccans use these specific tools as a symbolic representation of the Goddess and the God as well as the ways that we cast Magick and transform energy.

Each tool has a specific use, purpose, meaning, and effect upon your rituals, rites, ceremonies and spells and they can all be kept on your altar or in places in your house where you regularly make Magick. As with all matters Magickal, it is important that prior to using these tools that you spend time doing some kind of purification, consecration, and charging.

You don't have to do all at once, or all three together. I will usually only purify and cleanse my tools based on how much craftwork I am doing. Also, if I am doing really big and elaborate spells and rituals, I will usually purify the tools afterward so that by the next time I am ready to cast they will be good to go.

The tools are your cabinet for how you can begin to make your dreams become a reality. Tools direct energy and they harness it. They hold it close and they honor what you are invoking in your Magick. There are no specific rules to how you should or shouldn't use them or care for them. Use your best judgment and intuition in your personal practices.

Broom

The witch's broom is also known as a besom. Traditionally, it will be made from a large bundle of twigs, tied together in places to form a handle, leaving the bottom fanned out for sweeping. The besom acts as a purification tool and is used to sweep the circle and clear it of negative energy and vibration. It is also a traditional part of hand-fasting ceremonies (marriage union) in which the bride and groom will jump over the broom.

There is also, of course, the classic imagery of a witch flying across the moon on her besom, but we all know that that is just a fairytale about witchcraft...or is it?

Cords Of Color

A cord is also called a cingulum and it is simply just a length of rope that is often worn as a belt in the Wiccan tradition. A cord is typically given to a new initiate and the color will sometimes signify the rank of the coven member, but not always. Gardner considered it one of the three main tools that must always be available during rituals, along with the athame and the censer.

For the solitary practitioner, cords need not be only about holding your robe and signifying your rank.

They are also tools to help you measure things, as well as for uses in binding Magickal or tying knots for Magickal purposes and uses. It is good to have a good length of cord around for these purposes in your rituals and spells.

Censer

A censer is an ornate, or simple, tool to contain incense. It usually hangs from a chain or a cord so it can be swung back and forth, wafting the smoke from the incense in order to purify the space. Many modern witches will use herb bundles, smudge sticks, and incense cones instead, but the traditional censer is very good for loose incenses and resins and has a very pleasant feeling when you rhythmically walk it around a space in swinging motion.

Essentially, the act of using the censer is to purify the area and make it more inviting to the deities being invoked. You can certainly supplement the use of a censer with other incense and desirous foods for your God and Goddess.

Wand

The wand can be used to represent either Air or Fire, depending on which path of Wicca you are asking. In the Tarot Deck, the Wands are associated with Fire, and the Swords are related to Air. It really depends on your intuitive practices what feels right for you. Wands are typically made of wood and can also be made of crystal, stone, or other natural materials. Many witches will personalize their wands by carving sacred symbols into them, or painting and decorating them.

The wand is a tool to help you direct the energy of your spells and evocations. It can be substituted for your athame if you prefer the softer edge and quality of the wand. It is a tool to call upon the higher dimensional life forms, like fairies and angels, who would likely feel a lot more welcome if there wasn't a sword or a blade commanding their entry. A wand casts a direct request of invitation but is far less fierce.

Chalice

The chalice is a representation of the Goddess and her sacred womb or the womb of all life in the cosmos. It is most commonly used to contain the drink offerings to the Goddess, most commonly wine, but alcohol is not a requirement of practicing Wicca. It is also associated with the West and the waters of life.

In the Great Rite, the chalice is the energy of the divine feminine that copulates with the masculine sword, or athame. The chalice receives the blade to symbolize their sacred union. In Gardnerian Wicca, it was connected to the concept of the Holy Grail, possessing the power of restorative life. A silver chalice is most common on the traditional altar, but you can get creative and fun and find the goblet that suits your personality and your practice. Taking a sip from it during rituals is a great way to expand your energy and welcome the energy of the deities.

Pentacle

A pentacle is really just a round disk with a symbol painted, drawn, or carved on it. The most common symbol drawn on the pentacle is the pentagram which is the sacred five-pointed star that represents all 5 elements. It is the representation of the earth element, grounding, and life-giving, as well as stable and protective. A pentacle laid flat with its sacred symbol on the surface is most often used for blessing and consecrating tools, as well as offerings to the deities, like food or objects. It can also be used for summoning spirits. It can be made out of a variety of materials like wood, clay, metal, etc.

Athame

The Athame is the blade that is about the size of a dagger or hunting knife. Some Wiccans will also keep a sword on hand for rituals and rites while others will just use the athame to represent the energy of the sword. It will typically represent the element of Fire in many traditions, or Air in other. In the traditional Tarot deck, the sword represents Air.

The athame is notoriously black-handled (although some paths of Wicca chose a white handle) and is double-edged. It can be used in place of the wand to cast your circle and to charge objects and other tools with energy. It is not a tool of violence and should never be used in a threatening way. It is purely for ritual and symbolic cutting of the cord and directing of energy. Some traditions state that if your athame ever draws blood it must be destroyed.

Cauldron

As you read in the history of Wicca and witchcraft in Chapter 1, the cauldron has long been viewed as a witch's tool, despite really just originating as a giant soup pot. They come in all different sizes and are also a representation of the sacred feminine womb where life comes to fruition and is born.

Cauldrons are fire-safe, meaning they can carry heat which is perfect for those witches who like to burn things for the spells. You can cast a lot of good Magick with a little cauldron fire and having even a small one on your altar will help you accomplish many spell and ritual tasks. In place of a censer, it can be a great way to burn loose incense, as well as a great place to burn away unwanted energies or to empower your spells with fire. It can also be used for mixing ingredients and brewing potions and elixirs.

Bell

A bell makes a beautiful sound and when chimed will bring all energies to attention. It is a call to focus and beginning your rituals as well as a marker of the endpoint. It is very awakening and simultaneously grounding energy. Depending on what it is being used for, it can be rung a specific number of times to raise the energy of your spell or ritual, as well as ask deities to enter your circle of magic. It is a very clear and direct call to the energy of all life. Having a bell tone you like is important so try a few different sizes and shapes to make sure you have the resonance you like for your Magick.

Book of Shadows

The Book of Shadows also called the Grimoire, is where you store all of your Wiccan and craft knowledge. It is your living journey of exploration of rituals, spells, and the craft. Your Book will be your go-to tool to hold the secrets to your practice and as your practice grows, so will your Book of Shadows.

The next chapter will detail everything you need to know about making your very own Book of Shadows and how to effectively organize it. You won't need to fill it all up right away. It is like a journal of Magick and will be added to overtime. Your Book of

Shadows will hold all of the recipes you need to practice your craft.

Chapter 11: How To Create Your Book Of Shadows

In Wicca, the Book of Shadows is the Holy book that lists everything you need to know about your craft. A coven will have a unique Book that belongs to all of the members and any new initiates will have to copy the coven's original book in order to keep the tradition alive. A solitary or eclectic practitioner will have their own unique version of a Book of Shadows, or Grimoire and will find ways to incorporate everything they are learning from their journey along the way.

There are a few key things to know to help you build your Book of Shadows in the best way. First off, what is a Book of Shadows and do you even need to have one? A Book of Shadows isn't just your spell book or your recipes for Magick. It contains all of the information you are collecting that is specific to your Magick practice. It certainly will contain all of the detailed noted for your rituals and spells, and it will also have a lot of your progress as you grow in your practice.

The Book will also be a place that you will be able to reference certain things. You may want to keep a dictionary of Runic symbols or the Ogham Alphabet in your Book. You can also have pages of devotion to your deities or sections about moon phases and how to coordinate your own Esbats properly. A Book of Shadows is your connection to your practice and it is a creative art that allows you to express what your practice actually is on paper.

So do you need one? Honestly, you don't have to have a Book of Shadows to be a Wiccan or practice witchcraft. You can certainly look up each spell or ritual one at a time as it is happening from other sources and you can also just eclectically plan things without a lot of organization if that is the kind of craft you are choosing to have.

All of your Magick is inside of you and you only need YOU to be a Wiccan and a witch. The Book of Shadows is a beautiful compliment to your practice and I recommend using one, especially in the beginning to help get you started and feeling organized. To help you understand how a Book is laid out, I have included a step-by-step guide to creating your own. You don't have to use or follow all of these steps. You can decide what you like the best and go from there.

Ways To Organize Your Book Of Shadows

First of all, when preparing to get started with creating your first Book of Shadows, you have to find the right book for yourself. There are so many shops and online stores that sell handmade Grimoires, totally blank and ready to be filled. Or you may take pleasure in the art and craft of book-binding and can make your own from your preferred materials and resources.

My first Book of Shadows was a bit of a mess because I wanted to keep adding to it. Looking back on my early days with Magick, I would have organized everything I wanted in it first in a scratch notebook and then carefully written in all of my spells, rituals and other details after I felt like my "first draft" was completed. You can go either way with it and it can be fun to go back and look at the things you have changed or altered in spells so you can see the evolution and progress of your journey with Magick. Think of it as a living extension of your craft.

When you have found the book that you want to hold your secret mysteries, you can prepare to add to it. Organizing it can seem a little daunting at first, but you can also just follow some of these helpful tips and ideas.

- Leave the first page empty until you are ready to consecrate it with your name. when you are ready to claim the book, on the first page you can write, "this is the magical book of shadows of [your name] begun this day, [date]"

- Determine sections of the book and mark the pages to begin each section. You may want a much thicker part of the book to be available to your spells and rituals, while other sections might only need enough pages to detail the Runic alphabet.

- Determine what sections you want to have in your book before you begin to write anything in it.

- Have additional paper that you like that fits well with the style of your book so you can add sheets of information as needed. I will often glue a new page into a section as it compliments an already existing page or acts as an elaboration on something in my Grimoire.

These are just a few handy tips to help you prepare for the next steps: what to include in your Book of Shadows.

Sections To Include In Your Book Of Shadows

Your book can be so many things and carry so much of the information about your unique practice. You can even include a lot of what you learned in this book already, including a history of Wicca and witchcraft, as well as various Wiccan paths and covens.

You can also just keep it really simple, and for the solitary practitioner, it really all depends on what your practice is focusing on. Some of the following sections would be a great place to start with organizing your Book of Shadows:

- **Rules To Live By**

   Having a section devoted to your personal craft rules will help you stay focused on maintaining your ethical code of Magick.

The Wiccan Rede and the Law of Three are an example of that and having a section that simply states what your purpose and intentions with Magick are is like having a mission statement. This section can be added to, like any other, and can begin simply.

- **Sabbats And Esbats**

  Having a section devoted to the Wheel of the Year will be of great benefit when you are organizing your celebrations, rituals, and altar decorations. In this section, you can incorporate the meaning of each cycle and season and what herbs, foods, beverages, and materials you might need for each time of the year. With the Esbats, you can include information about the moon phases and how to best celebrate each one, incorporating similar ideas for decorating your altar and preparing a moon feast.

- **Symbols And Correspondences**

  A section of symbols and correspondences acts as a very useful reference guide, especially when you are just getting started in your craft. It's a lot to memorize. Having a section that you can look at that will show you the different Runes and their meanings, different Celtic symbols, and otherworldly symbols, the Ogham alphabet, astrological correspondences, etc. will help you feel secure in your knowledge and having easy access to it will help you work with your craft more efficiently and effectively.

- **Herbal Magick, Candle Magick, Crystal Magick**

  Keeping a section of information about the various uses for each herb, candle, and crystal will be endlessly useful. You can have a different section for each one and incorporate your most frequently used, herbs and crystals. Candle Magick deals a lot with color and using symbols carved into the wax, or anointing them with herbs and oil. Sections for each and understanding the properties of all of them will help you immensely. I would recommend leaving extra pages available for adding herb and crystal identification. There are literally thousands out there to choose to get to know in your craft.

- **Spells**

What Book of Shadows would be complete without a section of spells? This section will be an easy and fun addition to your Book and can be added to as you learn new spells and invent your own. It is nice to have them organized by category as well, keeping all of your love spells separate from your money spells so that you can reference them more quickly. You can also include all of the steps to casting a spell that you learned in Chapter 9.

- **Crafts**

  crafts can actually be a part of spell casting, but you can keep a separate section with instructions for your crafts. This could include candle making, incense making, patterns for poppets and sachets or dream pillows, different types of knots you can tie, and so forth. The craft section will go well next to your spell section because more often than not when you are crafting, you are casting.

- **Recipes**

  Recipes are not to be confused with spells, although they have similar characteristics and can easily become part of your spell casting work. Recipes will be more along the lines of cooking, brewing, and stewing potions. They can be herbal tea infusions, sacred loaves of bread and treats for offerings to the Goddess and God, recipes for certain Sabbats and Esbats. The recipe section is your cookbook of magical foods, potions, brews, and anything fun for you to treat yourself with magically.

- **Chants, Prayers, Songs**

  Coming up with your chants, prayers, and songs is a very special feeling. You may like to find already existing song ideas and prayers, or you may want to exercise the muscles of your inner poet. Either way, having a section just for this is a good way to keep it organized.

- **A Dream Journal**

  A section to write your dreams down is an excellent addition to your Book of Shadows. The more you are practicing Magick and invoking the divine energies of Spirit, the more communication and astral travel you will experience in your dream world. You may receive important messages that need to be deciphered and having your dream journal handy to review your progress is a profound personal experience.

- **General Journal Section**

  In addition to a dream journal, a general journal section is a great way for you to mark important moments in your spiritual journey. It can feel like your Book is actually listening to you as if it has its own personality and presence in your life. When you have your Book to talk to, you can embrace the deeper mysteries of yourself and of the universe. It is a wonderful place of discovery and it is always another amazing journey when you go back and read what you have done before on your path.

Taking Care Of Your Book Of Shadows

Your Book of Shadows, like any other Magickal tool you use, needs to be cared for properly. It is your sacred book of Magick and needs to be treated like a close friend and ally and not like any other book you put on the shelf or toss on the table. Your Book of Shadows needs a special place to call home, whether that is on your altar, in a cupboard, in a drawer, or somewhere else sacred and Magickal. Here are some helpful tips to keep your book happy and in good condition:

- **Purify Your Book**

  Using a sage smudge stick, you can waft purifying smoke around your book and on its pages to keep it clear of any unwanted energy or negative forces. You can also draw a ring of salt around the book to keep it cleared and purified. This you can do on your altar or other sacred workspace and leave the book in the ring of salt for 1 hour to 24 hours.

- **Consecrate Your Book**

  Using other Magickal tools, you can imbue your book with the energy of the Goddess and god in a special ritual or ceremony. This can be a very special time for you to bond with your book. You can name it, decorate it, talk to it, and invite other energies to bless your book in your ritual.

- **Charge Your Book**

  You can use the power of the Sun and the Moon to help your book feel the fullness of the power of either celestial body. If you are desiring more feminine moon energy, you can display your book in a full moonlit window and let it absorb the power of the bright mother moon. If you need the God energy in your book, you can lay it in a sun patch throughout the day and let it connect to the powerful Sun energy. If you are comfortable with it, you can also set up an outdoor altar to perform this ritual.

Your Book of Shadows is your Magick on the page. It is a beautiful extension of your craft and it holds the secrets to your identity as a witch and a Wiccan. Take good care of this book and make it a part of your family. Give birth to it as soon as you are ready and let it show you how to make it the perfect Book of Shadows for your personal Magick.

One more thing that you can include in your Book of Shadows on the front page, is your dedication to your craft. The next chapter will give a brief overview of the dedication you make to your journey with Magick.

Chapter 12: Initiating One's Dedication To The Wiccan Path

With any spiritual practice, there is a space of questioning and learning before a true dedication comes to pass. Being born into a family of Wiccans and witches, I was never told I had to become what they are, but I was taught the lessons of the craft from a very young age. It wasn't until I was almost 20 years old that I finally decided I was ready to become dedicated to this craft and it was with a coven and not as a solitary.

It helps to understand and know the difference between Coven Initiation and Self-Dedication and in this chapter I will help you decide which way you might want to travel with Wicca. Overall, many who come to these practices are able to explore it and enjoy it for a time and while some are easily swept off into other spiritual realities and identities, others will feel a strong pull toward Wicca.

There are a lot of people practicing and dedicated to this path, while there are plenty of others who dabble with it and use it as a platform to enjoy a variety of other Pagan practices and rituals. Wicca is a way of life and so it can be a very important step to dedicate yourself to it. A coven is extremely different from practicing as a solitary and the initiation processes are equally different.

Coven Initiation

If you are interested in practicing with a coven, your initiation will be quite complex. Usually, you will be accepted as an initiate only after you have met all of the coven members and have been able to spend time together. A coven is like a family and the emotional energies of this bond run deep. It is important that everyone feels compatible together.

So the initial stages of initiation are kind of like a get-to-know-you phase. Once you have been accepted by the coven as a viable option as an initiate, you will then have to spend time being mentored by someone in the coven. All covens are different and these phases of time are unknown and vary widely from person to person and coven to coven. It can sometimes be a few weeks or months before you are considered "ready".

The ritual of initiation is very elaborate and incorporates all of the learning experiences leading up to the point that you are actually included through a ceremonial rite with the rest of the coven group. It can last for several hours and many covens are very secretive about all of the practices, So specific ritual steps are not always easy to come by unless you are a part of a coven.

Coven initiation is a very intense journey and it requires a lot of dedication and devotion to walking the Wiccan path. It is definitely not for anyone who is unsure about whether it is a good idea for them. And it will be a very close relationship with several other people where you will be expected to participate in every ritual and ceremony. It is a serious commitment to a group and that group's beliefs and practices of learning and initiation.

If you are not sure that a coven is the right path for you, there is always the solitary practice that involves a much less elaborate approach.

Self-Dedication

Self-Dedication can also be called self-initiation. It is really just the ritual of giving yourself to your craft with a full mind, body, and heart. Many solitary practitioners will say that you should practice for a year and a day before committing to this path. It is advisable to spend some quality time on this journey before you choose it as a way of life. A year offers you all of the Sabbats and Esbats you need to appreciate the Wheel of the Year which is the backbone of Wicca.

Another suggestion of self-dedication is that you perform your ritual on a New Moon, which is the moment of new beginning, possibility, and growth. These are just suggestions of course and every witch is unique, so keep that in mind and trust your intuition and spiritual guidance.

There are so many pleasurable ways that you can dedicate yourself to the Wiccan path and I will offer you one possible guide to the solitary self-initiation process. You can perform this skyclad (in the nude) or in clothing, it is up to you. You can also decide if you want to give yourself a new, Magickal name that you will use in your rituals and private practice. You will want to have an altar set up somewhere and all you really need is a white candle, blessing oil, and a white sage smudge stick.

1. Begin by taking a purification bath.

2. After your bath, come to the place where you will perform your ritual.

3. Cast a circle of Magick and sit inside of it.

4. Light the white candle and relax in your rituals space.

5. Purify your body, your candle and your oil with the sage smoke.

6. Use the oil to anoint your forehead, your eyelids, your cheeks, lips, throat, and heart. You can also anoint the palms of your hands and the souls of your feet.

7. Speak words of dedication as they feel right to you. It will be a very personal journey and so choosing the verbiage that resonates with your path is key. An example is: I bless my forehead with this blessing oil, I am one with my power and the power of the God and Goddess. So mote it be.

8. You can spend some time speaking to the divine about your desires for your practice, your dedication to your role as a Wiccan, and

your presence within yourself to be a Magick force of positive light.

9. When your dedication is complete, close your circle.

You can make your ritual so much more elaborate, which is why it is important to remember that these are just guidelines and tools to help you get started. Being a witch is an intuitive journey and you want to give yourself the creativity to perform the ritual of self-initiation that is super special for you.

You can add flowers and herbs and make a special outfit for the occasion. You can decorate your body however you like and enjoy sacred foods and beverages in the circle while you celebrate your dedication. It is all about you and what you would like to explore with your craft.

You can also remember that you are in a great spiral of rebirth and what you are doing now to dedicate yourself to this path has happened before and will happen again. Wiccans believe in reincarnation and as you are initiating yourself into your path, you can engage with the idea that your soul memory already knows what to do and has always known. You are living here and now as yourself and empowering your beliefs to embrace that you will live another life as a witch. And so it is!

The last chapter will expand upon the concept of reincarnation and help you recognize that everything you do to dedicate yourself to this path now, will revisit you again in your next life. It is truly a powerful cycle of existence.

Chapter 13:
The Spiral Of Rebirth

The life that you live is not the only life you perceive, at least that is one of the main philosophies of Wicca. Reincarnation is a taboo subject in quite a lot of religious circles and ideologies, and if you aren't sure what it means to be reincarnated, allow me to enlighten you.

In Wicca, the belief is that your soul goes through many lives in order to grow and learn lessons. One life just isn't enough to accomplish perfection and enlightenment and so we must go through many iterations of "self" in order to accomplish this goal. The lives that you live are fraught with difficulties and challenges that you set up before you even come back to Earth so that you have a path to walk and a new set of lessons to discover and learn from.

The general understanding is that there really isn't a heaven or hell, or any forces of judgment to disregard you at the end of your life if you didn't do a "good job". The places that you go between your embodied lives are different depending on each tradition of Wicca.

Some Wiccans believe in Summerland which is an idyllic resting place covered in grassy fields and flowers, an Eden to prepare for your next life. Others believe that it is far less physical and is more of an energetic whirlpool in which we come together with all of the other ancient celestials and deities as we prepare for our next course.

There are a lot of different ideas on the matter and as you celebrate your path with Wicca, you can learn more about what it is that resonates most with you about the in-between realms of your soul. Reincarnation is also wrapped up in the concept of karma which plays a big part in your journey in this life influencing your journey in the next. It also relates to a karmic past and having to learn from the karma of other lives while you are still learning lessons on your present course.

Karma is a way for you to treat your life with reverence as well as the lives of others as you are traveling through your soul experience. It is the mark of an evolved soul who can let others walk the path that they must to learn the lessons of their own incarnation while you do the same. Reincarnation is what allows us to ascend further into our highest forms of self and allows us to see the great beyond as we become higher and higher in vibration.

As you embrace your Wiccan path, remind yourself that you have been here before and chances are you have already studied these Magick ways and lived by these standards of existence already. You will find all of your soulful life experiences laid out before you like a shimmering path of deeper knowing and truth when you let yourself follow your heart and teach yourself the ways of the craft.

Continue your journey with love in your heart and reverence for all things for it will follow you into your next life and inform you of what lessons you are ready to learn again. The reality of right now is the reality of what was and what will be, so live your life fully, celebrate nature, cast your spells, spin your Magick web, and embrace your true power and path as a Wiccan. So mote it be!

Conclusion

Wicca is a powerful way of life. It is an essential reality that can bring you so much inner harmony, peace, abundance, fertility, and prosperity on all levels of your life. You can give great thanks to the life that you have as we are all here to live and seek our truth with the Great Mother and the Father Sky, held by the universe as we explore our eternal destinies and practice knowing who we are from deep within the blanket of Magickal truth.

I am here to give you all of that faith in yourself and knowledge of the Wiccan path so that you can further your own Magick and self-discovery. I hope that you have found the information that you needed to inspire an even deeper existence within the craft you are creating in your life.

Let these ideas, teachings, guidelines, and tutorials help you gain the confidence you need to support a fully alive and awakened Wiccan practice of your own. You are your true power and to worship the divine in all things is the essence of wholeness within your life and yourself.

As you move forward on your journey, continue to teach yourself new concepts, histories, methodologies, and transformations to help you build your practice into the work of art it is destined to be. Let your intuition be your guide and give you all of the courage you need to fulfill your dreams of Magick.

Asking for what you want in this life is part of embracing your own divine, eternal Magick life force and I want you to go forward carrying the purpose of living to your fullest through the Wiccan experience. You can make manifest all that you are wanting to know in your life through the Magick you create and that is the main take away from this book. As long as you are willing to communicate with the divine and with your own highest self, you will find what you are looking for and Wiccan Magick is a pathway to getting there.

Anything you do from here forward will be a gift to getting yourself on track with your own spells, rituals, altar space, Book of Shadows and daily practices. There is such abundance in this way of life and so many ways to enjoy it. You can be truly crafty and creative with your work and your inner world to bring more harmony into your life, the second main take away from this book.

The final takeaway is that Wicca brings you into divine connection with all of the energies of the universe. It shows you that we all have a significant part to play in the energy of all creation and that as you practice your rituals and spells, you are declaring that you are present and available to live your life through Magick and awareness of all that is around you.

Take these lessons to heart and do with them what you will. Harm none and remember the Rule of Three. Let the blessings of life unfold through the seasons along with the cycles of the Sun and Moon. Give thanks to the wind, the water, the heat of the fire, and the firm soil underfoot. Breathe Magick into your life every day and ask to know what you must in order to keep growing in your powerful path of Magick. So Mote It Be!

And finally, please offer an honest review of this book on Amazon if you feel it has given value to your life and your exploration of the Wiccan path.

Blessings!

www.ingramcontent.com/pod-product-compliance
Lightning Source LLC
La Vergne TN
LVHW011006200726
843509LV00011B/1015